Educating

for

Eco-Justice

and

Community

C. A. Bowers

The University of Georgia Press   *Athens & London*

Set in 10.3 on 15 Minion

Printed digitally in the United States of America

Library of Congress Cataloging-in-Publication Data

Bowers, C. A.

Educating for eco-justice and community / C. A. Bowers.

xi, 232 p. ; 23 cm.

Includes bibliographical references (p. 213–218) and index.

ISBN 0-8203-2305-5 (alk. paper) — ISBN 0-8203-2306-3
(pbk. : alk. paper)

1. Environmental education. 2. Environmental justice.

I. Title.

GE70 .B682 2001

363.7'0071—dc21   2001027288

Paperback ISBN-13: 978-0-8203-2306-0

British Library Cataloging-in-Publication Data available

Contents

Preface

The main thesis of this book is that the social justice issues of class, race, and gender need to be framed in terms of a more comprehensive theory of eco-justice. Unfortunately, the followers of Dewey and Freire, as well as the theorists inspired by Ilya Prigogine and Alfred North Whitehead, continue to frame their recommendations for educational reform in ways that ignore the cultural roots of the ecological crisis. The various approaches these educational theorists take in conceptualizing how educational reform can alleviate social injustices contain a double bind. Their view of social justice, which is couched in the Enlightenment language of emancipation of the individual, involves achieving equal standing in a culture that is overshooting the sustaining capacity of natural systems. The double bind is in the fact that the cultural groups most directly affected by contaminated environments and the loss of employment opportunities due to the "outsourcing" connected with a global economy are the minorities most in need of eco-justice. These marginalized cultural groups also face the loss of traditions essential to their identity and forms of community through the cultural homogenization that accompanies a hyper-consumer culture. Reform efforts that contribute to eco-justice must address the right of future generations to inhabit an environment that has not been diminished by the greed and materialism of the current generation. The need for non-Western cultures to attain a more adequate material standard of living without being forced to adopt the Western model of development must also be considered in an eco-justice pedagogy.

The above summary involves a shift in conceptual categories that needs to be made explicit. Issues of race, class, and gender are usually examined from a sociological perspective that utilizes, as its moral norm, the idea of equality—in terms of the law and economic and educational opportunities, and in the political arena. This is an important moral norm guiding educational reform. Unfortunately, the ideal of equality, especially when framed in terms of assumptions that represent the individual as the basic social unit, does not take account of differences in cultural ways of knowing. The sociological literature has yet to address this crucial issue.

The attempt to avoid the reified and thus too easily universalized categories of sociology by adopting an anthropological perspective can lead to another set of misunderstandings—especially since the word *culture* also has a long history of distorted reifications. The dangers of adopting an essentialist way of thinking that represents the members of a culture as embracing a common set of beliefs and values that sets them off from other supposedly closed cultural systems are very real. The anthropological perspective has also led to a politics of domination. The cultural assumptions encoded in the approaches some anthropologists have taken to explain the nature of culture, as well as the reifying characteristics of the printed word and the museum setting, have contributed to a popular misunderstanding that ignores how the lived patterns encompassed by the word *culture* are dynamic in ways that involve individualized expression, taken-for-granted patterns, exogenous and endogenous sources of change, and different temporal patterns. The use of the term *hybrid culture* (García Canclini 1995) represents an attempt to account for these dynamic and syncretistic characteristics. As that is an exceedingly awkward phrase, I will continue to use the word *culture,* but in an inclusive way that takes account of the total range of life world experiences: shared patterns and traditions, interpretations that reflect biographically distinct and group-based experiences, movement into and between different symbolic spaces that have their own norms of behavior and thought, layers of metaphorical constructions that reproduce the thought patterns of past elite groups, tensions and continuities between empowering and destructive traditions, and the antitradition traditions of modernity as expressed in science, technology, and hyperconsumerism.

In addition, culture must be understood as encompassing the divergent ways of knowing and the value systems encoded in the languaging patterns of different cultural groups—even as their youth wear Nikes and the older people watch American television programs. One of the primary reasons why I retain the word *culture* is that it provides a basis for challenging the modern myth of the autonomous individual. To make this point another way: the use of the word *culture* is essential to challenging the proclivity of modern elites to universalize their categories of thinking—including their prescriptions for reform. It is also essential to the argument that the language of different cultural groups may encode the intergenerational knowledge of the sustainable characteristics of their bioregion. For example, when a language that previously carried forward the intergenerational knowledge of the medicinal properties of local plants ceases to be spoken by the younger generation, local practices that previously were the basis of self-sufficiency are replaced by consumerism—which creates new forms of dependencies and impoverishment. This important insight of Ivan Illich has been largely ignored because it could not be reconciled with the modern ideal of development (which has made consumerism the ultimate virtue).

There is another possible source of confusion that needs to be addressed. At different points in my analysis I use the concept of *double bind* to explain how what appears to be a progressive development may contribute to destructive consequences that generally go unrecognized. As an example of a double bind, Gregory Bateson cites the old European test for determining if an individual was guilty of witchcraft. The suspected witch was tied to the end of a plank that was then immersed in water. The person who sank (and thus drowned) was presumed to be innocent; the person who floated was found to be guilty—and then burned at the stake (Bateson and Bateson 1987:173). The only way out of the double bind was to question the guiding assumptions—which could not be done in that atmosphere of fear and superstition. Today there are double binds in shopping online and at the local Wal-Mart, which is convenient for the individual but undermines the local economy and systems of mutual dependency, and in the globalization of Western technologies. Unlike Bateson's example, in which a single individual was harmed, the consequences of not being able to recognize the cultural assumptions that give rise to double bind behaviors and ways of thinking will be experienced more widely and will put more lives (indeed whole cultures) at risk.

Recognizing the double binds inherent in "progressive" educational reform proposals leads to the understanding that change is not always the manifestation of a linear form of progress. Indeed, how educational reforms contribute to strengthening ecologically problematic cultural patterns may not even be recognized. The double bind inherent in a form of material progress that undermines the viability of life-sustaining natural systems can easily be understood when stated in this explicit way, but the linguistic/

conceptual conventions that contribute to this double bind are generally taken for granted and thus not made explicit. The underlying assumptions may even be encoded in the "god-words" that cannot be challenged because of the danger of being seen as opposing social progress. In the following chapters I identify how the metaphors of leading educational theorists are based on a view of progress that is being used to globalize an individual- and consumer-centered culture. The irony is that many of these educational theorists represent themselves as critics of capitalism and the growing dominance of technology—which is yet another example of a double bind. Their view of emancipation, and the deep cultural assumptions it is based on, undermines the forms of knowledge and networks of mutual support that are the basis of more self-sufficient lifestyles and communities. I will also point out the double bind inherent in their reified political categories.

The intellectual pathway I have taken in recent years has been influenced by graduate students at the University of Oregon and Portland State University, by colleagues in different parts of the world who shared their ideas and pointed me toward scholarly sources that I had overlooked, and by the writings of educational theorists who have ignored the ecological crisis. Indeed, I have probably learned the most from the latter group—but it has not been the form of learning that has turned me into a follower. As in the case of past books, I must also acknowledge the many sources of encouragement and suggestions for improving the clarity of my writing given by Mary Katharine Bowers.

Educating
for
Eco-Justice
and
Community

Introduction

Over the last decades of the twentieth century a number
of writers explained how public schools and universities contribute
to the patterns of inequality in society. They even suggested broad
reforms in curriculum and pedagogy that were more the embodiment of their own deep desire for social justice than a realistic
assessment of the interest or ability of educators to use the classroom to effect radical changes in American society. Indeed, the
call for public schools and universities to become catalysts for
social change is a dominant characteristic of what can be called
the "messianic" tradition in American education. Many of these
proposals for harnessing the nation's educational institutions to the
task of achieving social justice for all citizens were not adequately
grounded in an understanding of the structural characteristics
of society. That is, no matter how effective the teachers and no
matter how empowering the curriculum, the educational process
lacked the political means necessary to transform the controlling
political and economic interests. Other proposals, in spite of the
good intentions they embodied, did not take into account most

educators' reluctance to question the prevailing assumptions and values that make it so easy to give lip-service to the ideals of social justice while reinforcing the patterns of thinking that perpetuate the problem.

This book faces the same challenges that undermined the efforts of previous advocates of using the classroom to "build a new social order"—to borrow the visionary statement of an earlier progressive thinker. It too may fail to convince public school teachers and university professors of the seriousness of the structural and conceptual/moral problems we face as a society and as citizens of the Earth's ecosystems. It will certainly lack the political and economic muscle that multinational corporations and national governments possess and use to dictate changes that serve their interests. Nevertheless, the difference between this book and earlier efforts to promote educational reform may be great enough to warrant withholding any comparison with the largely failed efforts of the past.

As I explain in the following chapters, social justice advocates such as John Dewey and Paulo Freire, as well as more contemporary theorists, base their analyses and educational recommendations on a view of society that fails to acknowledge a crucial point: at the deep symbolic level, not all cultural groups in American society share the modern understanding of the Enlightenment ideals of progress and individual freedom. Their analyses also fail to take account of the scale and rate of changes occurring in the Earth's ecosystems. While the current pattern of framing social justice issues in terms of the categories of race, gender, and class is highly useful for some analyses, the arguments for what constitutes a morally just society are still being framed in terms of the Western, high-status way of thinking that represents the individual as the basic social unit. Indeed, at the core of these analyses is an interlocking set of culturally specific assumptions that have gone largely unquestioned. Also unnoticed is that as the individual members of marginalized groups—women, ethnic minorities, the underemployed, and the working class—overcome social barriers and thus achieve greater parity in the economic and political life of the community, they most often *join* rather than alter the dominant pathway of cultural development. That is, they become participants in the consumer- and technology-oriented society. While I am not arguing that anyone should be denied the materialistic opportunities that the members of mainstream culture take for granted, it is important to note that the achievement of a greater measure of social justice in the spheres of education, the marketplace, and the political arena can contribute to other forms of social injustice.

For example, advocates of educational reform fail to recognize that any definition of social justice that does not take account of how human demands on the natural environment are affecting the lives of future generations is fundamentally flawed. Indeed, it seems incomprehensible to write about social justice for women, minorities, and the economic underclass without considering the ways in which the Earth's ecosystems are being rapidly degraded. Nor should any discussion of social justice be framed in a way that ignores how achieving greater access to the material standard of living that is today's measure of personal success depends on market forces that are appropriating the resources of non-Western cultures and displacing their traditional forms of knowledge. Unlike ecofeminist writers, the educational proponents of empowering marginalized groups have also ignored the fact that the scale of chemical changes in natural systems resulting from modern technologies is undermining the physical health and shortening the life spans of many people. This fact has not, however, been lost on members of minority communities who have been organizing themselves to resist the chemical contamination of their local environments. An extensive body of research shows that the victims of long-standing patterns of marginalization are the most adversely affected by the toxic by-products of consumer society. As these findings are often reported in the popular media, it is difficult to understand why the concern with the declining viability of the Earth's ecosystems has not been recognized as an essential aspect of any educational theorist's discussion of social justice.

My own experience of being labeled a reactionary thinker by educational theorists who want social justice issues framed *only* in terms of the categories of race, gender, and class serves as a constant reminder that the theorists who view themselves as agents of radical social change are themselves reproducing the conceptual patterns of the past. Because they use traditional ways of framing social justice issues, they fail to recognize that addressing the cultural basis of the deepening ecological crisis is fundamental to any vision of social justice. The combined myths of anthropocentrism and the linear view of progress, which are still part of the mythopoetic basis of current thinking about emancipating subjugated groups, have led generations of progressive reformers to ignore the growing evidence of environmental degradation. Educational theorists who write today about social justice issues in ways that ignore the long-term implications of the ecological crisis are simply carrying forward this tradition of double bind thinking.

The argument that educational reform should be based on an understanding of what constitutes eco-justice should not be interpreted to mean that the poverty and limited opportunity for self and community development now experienced on a disproportionate scale by certain groups in American society should be ignored or downgraded in importance. Rather, reform should be viewed within a more inclusive category of analysis, one that makes visible both the double binds and the possibilities that educators have ignored in the past. An eco-justice-based approach also takes account of fundamental realities that cannot be dismissed as mere social constructions or matters of individual interpretation. The extreme weather patterns that accompany global warming are undeniably real. As is a global economic system that is based on fossil fuels and synthetic chemicals that are changing the biology of life, increasing illness and premature death in humans, and contributing to the extinction of more than ten thousand species a year (a conservative estimate). As people dependent on once abundant fisheries can attest, the degraded state of the marine ecosystems is leading not only to the loss of jobs but also to the loss of a vital source of food. The loss of topsoil (estimated at twenty-four billion tons annually, or what amounts over a ten-year period to 7 percent of the Earth's most productive agricultural land) becomes an especially significant "reality" when viewed in light of the rapid increase in the world population. The concurrent globalization of technologies that are narrowing the genetic basis of the food supply puts the world's population even further at risk. Similarly, we need to take into account the pattern of thinking that leads to disposing of toxic wastes in regions of the world where the interests of local populations are being ignored.

The downward trend in the viability of ecological systems is being disregarded by a public that wants to believe in the media and in shopping mall images of plenitude rather than consider the ecological consequences of their consumer lifestyle and their complicity in supporting the myths surrounding its globalization. Also ignored are the forms of knowledge being lost in different regions of the world—knowledge built up over generations of learning about the possibilities and limits of local ecosystems. The knowledge of cultural groups anchored in an intergenerational experience of place is being undermined through the introduction of Western media and other symbols of modernization. Multinational corporations are beginning to claim patent rights on local people's knowledge of biodiversity—thus further commodifying Nature and forcing local populations to become increasingly dependent on the marketplace to meet basic needs. Included in the loss of cultural diversity are the codes of moral reciprocity that served to limit human impact on natural systems. Traditional skills, customs, and codes of moral reciprocity that enable cultural groups to keep market relationships from becoming the dominant characteristic of community life are also disappearing under the pressure of modernization and economic development. The decline in the self-sufficiency of traditional communities, however, has not always been accompanied by the disappearance of cultural practices that are viewed as morally reprehensible in the West.

An eco-justice pedagogy must be based on a vocabulary that is able to represent the strengths and limitations of these traditional cultures as well as articulate what modern, urban cultural groups can learn from them *(which is profoundly different from borrowing from them)*. It must also clarify the double binds that characterize how many educational theorists have framed social justice issues—particularly the deep cultural assumptions that provided conceptual and moral legitimation for the Industrial Revolution. That individuals need to become emancipated from the hold of tradition is one of these assumptions. Ironically, this assumption is common to the thinking of Dewey and his contemporary followers, as well as to advocates of cyberbase communities such as Bill Gates, Sherry Turkle, and Esther Dyson. Other cultural assumptions that have influenced how educational theorists understand social justice issues include thinking of life processes (including the development of cultures) as evolutionary in nature—that is, moving from simple and primitive to complex and better adapted; anthropocentrism—which shows up in thinking about human possibilities in ways that do not recognize the dependence of humans on the viability of the environment; and viewing the individual as the basic social unit and thus the center of subjective decision making about what is of immediate interest.

The spread of the Industrial Revolution depended on the acceptance of these assumptions; indeed, they continue to be the basis of a modern and progressive lifestyle. The Industrial Revolution, that juggernaut of commodifying energy, would not now be entering its digital phase of development if the face-to-face traditions of community had not first been undermined by a modern ideology that combines the myths of individualism and linear social progress. The new technologies that allow elites to extend the commodification process make it all the more imperative that the double binds still present in the thinking of many educational reformers not be incorporated into how we think about the nature of an eco-justice pedagogy.

The presence of these conceptual and moral double binds is more than a matter of perpetuating the deep cultural patterns of thought that are the basis of deadly economic and technological practices. These double binds also limit the educator's ability to reform the curriculum in ways that lead to a regeneration of the traditions of interdependence within different communities—including their awareness of environmental limits. An eco-justice pedagogy should have as its main focus the recovery of the capacity of different cultural groups to sustain traditions that contribute to self-sufficiency, mutual support, and symbolic expression. In short, it should stress relationships and skills that make dependence on consumerism less necessary. What must be reversed is the way basic needs in health, nurturing, education, entertainment, leisure, work, community relationships, and so forth are increasingly defined and met by the purveyors of commodities and expert systems. Traditionally, many cultural groups were able to meet these needs in ways that did not damage the environment. Today, products and services are designed to create a continued state of dependency on the market-place. The commodification of children's play is one example of this transformation. Instead of children using personal imagination, exploring the possibilities of the local environment, and learning from their interactions with older children, play today is largely dictated by the design departments of major corporations that connect toys to brand-name images appearing in television commercials and megamovies such as *Star Wars* and *Jurassic Park*. In effect, toys have become the early stage of socialization to a state of dependency as well as the fantasy narratives and environments that support it.

With the exception of ethnic minorities who consciously strive to keep their traditions alive (even when they live within mainstream society), most modern communities have been reduced to anomic individuals and remnants of the nuclear family that are increasingly focused on meeting the rising cost of buying what previously was attained through personal skill and mutual effort within the household. The majority of social interactions now occur within the workplace, in consumer-related behavior, and in front of the television set—which is industry's pipeline for sending its consciousness-shaping messages and images. There are efforts within some communities to reverse this trend through non-commodified service organizations, youth sports programs, and public school and church-related activities. In addition, mentoring, community theater and other forms of artistic performance, and intergenerational sharing of skills and knowledge relating to a wide range of interests and needs represent just a few of the efforts being made to resist the growing pressure to become dependent on technology, consumerism, and outside experts.

The elements of community that continue to be undermined by consumer society's relentless efforts to expand the need to purchase goods and services is put in historical perspective in Kirkpatrick

Sale's study of the Luddites' resistance to the early phase of the Industrial Revolution. Of particular interest is his summary of the aspects of community that had to be transformed in order to expand markets and thus keep the production lines running at full tilt:

> All that "community" implies—self-sufficiency, mutual aid, morality in the marketplace, stubborn tradition, regulation by custom, organic knowledge instead of mechanistic science—had to be steadily and systematically disrupted and displaced. *All the practices that kept the individual from becoming a consumer had to be done away with so that the cogs and wheels of an unfettered machine called "the economy" could operate without interference, influenced merely by invisible hands and inevitable balances and all the rest of the benevolent free-market system.* (Sale 1995:38; italics added)

To paraphrase Sale in a way that illuminates how this process operates today: all the traditions that enable individuals, educational institutions, social organizations, and small businesses to keep from becoming dependent on the computer industry have to be represented in the public mind as outmoded, backward, and inefficient—with the most emphasis on the last metaphor, which now stands for a social pathology.

While the use of technology and other consumer items cannot be judged in dichotomous categories of good and bad, *unnecessary* dependence on meeting needs through products and services that can be purchased has disruptive consequences that weaken the viability of the family, community, and environment. Products and services require turning the environment into resources and then, at the end of the production-use cycle, returning degraded material and toxic wastes to the environment. The more that needs are met through the self-reliant capacities of individuals, families, and communities, the fewer the adverse impacts on the environment. There is another destructive cycle that accompanies the increasing reliance on consumerism. The more people rely on consumerism, the more they have to work in order to pay for their expanding dependencies: food preparation, entertainment, transportation, clothes, leisure time, health care, and so forth. And the more people have to work, the less time they have for parenting and involvement in activities that strengthen the reciprocal networks within the community.

Taking seriously the traditions within communities (which will vary among cultural groups, of course) that make their members less dependent on the marketplace brings into question educational theorists' practice of framing social justice issues within the conceptual and moral framework of liberalism—an "antitradition tradition" that coevolved with the Industrial Revolution. While the liberal animus toward all traditions and the simultaneous embrace of the myth of progress are celebrated in our educational institutions as the deepest expressions of contemporary wisdom, they contribute to an inability to discriminate between constructive, vital traditions and traditions that are destructive and the sources of injustice.

There is another dimension to an eco-justice pedagogy that has implications for curriculum reform at all levels of education. While I personally think that the current disparity in the distribution of wealth in American society, and between the North and the South, equals the ecological crisis in importance, I doubt that the educational process can have a direct ameliorative effect. Classroom discussions of the complicity of multinational corporations in the ecology of rich and poor may influence, down the road, how legislation is framed. But the ability of wealth to distort the democratic process in ways that favor the interests of the multinational corporations and other elite groups is too overwhelming for the educational process to have much real influence. In fact, such discussions are likely to leave many students with a feeling of utter powerlessness, and thus disinclined to become involved in the political process. While students need to understand the political behavior of Exxon, Dow Chemical, Microsoft, and other megacorporations, class discussions of poverty at the local level are more likely to have a direct effect. That is, an eco-justice pedagogy should address the causes of poverty and the creation of wealth at the community level, which requires an understanding of how to regenerate the sense of local responsibility and mutual support that has been undermined by national and international market forces.

Wendell Berry's essay "Conserving Communities" lists seventeen suggestions for improving the economic well-being and self-sufficiency of local communities. His guidelines can be used as a starting point for understanding how an eco-justice pedagogy can have a direct impact that goes beyond classroom discussions that too often have little lasting influence.

1. Always ask of any proposed change or innovation: What will this do to our community? How will this affect our common wealth?

2. Always include local nature—the land, the water, the air, the native creatures—within the membership of the community.

3. Always ask how local needs might be supplied from local sources, including the mutual help of neighbors.

4. Always supply local needs first (and only then think of exporting products—first to nearby cities, then to others).

5. Understand the ultimate unsoundness of the industrial doctrine of "labor saving" if that implies poor work, unemployment, or any kind of pollution or contamination.

6. Develop properly scaled value-adding industries for local products to ensure that the community does not become merely a colony of the national or global economy.

7. Develop small-scale industries and businesses to support the local farm and/or forest economy.

8. Strive to produce as much of the community's own energy as possible.

9. Strive to increase earnings (in whatever form) within the community for as long as possible before they are paid out.

10. Make sure that money paid into the local economy circulates within the community and decrease expenditures outside the community.

11. Make the community able to invest in itself by maintaining its properties, keeping itself clean (without dirtying some other place), caring for its old people, and teaching its children.

12. See that the old and the young take care of one another. The young must learn from the old, not necessarily and not always in school. There must be no institutionalized child care and no homes for the aged. The community knows and remembers itself by the association of old and young.

13. Account for costs now conventionally hidden or externalized. Whenever possible, these must be debited against monetary income.

14. Look into the possible uses of local currency, community-funded loan programs, systems of barter, and the like.

15. Always be aware of the economic value of neighborly acts. In our time, the costs of living are greatly increased by the loss of neighborhood, which leaves people to face their calamities alone.

16. A rural community should always be acquainted and interconnected with community-minded people in nearby towns and cities.

17. A sustainable rural community will depend on urban consumers loyal to local products. Therefore, we are talking about an economy that will always be more cooperative than competitive. (Berry 1996:413–415)

While Berry tends to think of the local community in terms of rural environments, many of his suggestions have both direct and indirect implications for urban settings. In fact, many ethnically conscious communities in urban areas have, partly out of necessity and partly as an expression of cultural tradition, been pursuing Berry's guidelines. The failure to include them as part of the public school and university curricula represents one of the ways in which our educational institutions perpetuate the further creation of wealth at the top rather than nurturing at the grassroots level both material and social forms of wealth.

An eco-justice pedagogy that addresses the curricular implications of Berry's guidelines for greater community self-reliance and economic well-being must also address another social justice issue: namely, the marginalization of the talent and skills of people who do not undertake some form of higher education. Equating higher education with the forms of knowledge needed to advance the national and global economy makes it more difficult for people to earn an income from their natural talents and communally acquired skills. Just as the wisdom of communal and environmental relationships is undermined by the expert knowledge learned in universities, the forms of knowledge and skill valued by corporations undermine the knowledge and skills vital to the noncommodified aspects of local communities. Read the educational goals that corporations and legislatures are now setting for public schools and universities to assess the truth of this generalization. Spokespersons for corporations want students to learn problem solving and how to think and write clearly; they want them to be mathematically literate and able to engage in group processes. Noticeably absent from their list of educational goals are the skills and knowledge needed for leading less commodified lives.

My emphasis on eco-justice as the inclusive conceptual and moral framework for guiding educational and, by extension, social reform is supported by the growing involvement of minority communities in addressing environmental issues. Ethnic and working-class communities are becoming increasingly active in the Citizen's

Clearinghouse for Hazardous Wastes, a network of more than 7,500 grassroots groups in or near communities where toxic waste–producing industries such as Union Carbide and Georgia-Pacific most often locate. Poor, marginalized, and politically weak communities are seen as offering less resistance to the environmental destruction and human suffering that accompanies such manufacturing facilities. This perception, which is strengthened by the "not-in-my-backyard" attitude of the more affluent and politically potent middle class, is also shared by the members of state legislatures and local bureaucrats who grant the siting permits to corporations.

The "not-in-my-backyard" attitude is now also growing within minority communities, however. It is based on living with the consequences of toxic wastes moving from the manufacturing facility into the local water supply, the food chain, and the air that people breathe. Thus, minorities' concern with environmental justice goes beyond issues of equal access to educational and employment opportunities and equal representation of their cultural achievements. Environmental justice, for them, has to do with not being overrepresented in the statistics on cancer deaths, birth deformities, and debilitating illnesses that lead to even deeper levels of poverty.

The arguments these minority groups are making for environmental justice are similar to the argument I have made over the years that environmental issues must have primacy in thinking about educational reform. The way *environment* was defined by the delegates to the First Nation of People of Color Environmental Leadership Summit, held in 1991 in Washington, D.C., and which continues to meet annually, makes this point even more cogently. The three hundred delegates, representing African, Native American, Latino, and Asian American communities, defined the environment as the "totality of life conditions in our communities—air and water, safe jobs for all at decent wages, housing, education, health care, humane prisons, equity, justice" (Szasz 1994:151–152). The last of the Principles of Environmental Justice the delegates defined in their preamble concludes with the statement that "environmental justice requires that we, as individuals, make personal and consumer choices to consume as little of Mother Earth's resources and to produce as little waste as possible; and make the conscious decision to challenge and re-prioritize our lifestyles to insure the health of the natural world for present and future generations" (Schwab 1994:443; see Appendix). How to transform this principle into the realities of individual, family, and community practices should be the primary concern of educators.

Why educators writing on social justice have ignored grassroots efforts to reverse the environmental damage experienced by poor and marginalized communities is a question that deserves serious consideration. Individuals who mobilize their communities to challenge environmental hazards are usually also skilled in attracting media attention—often at the national level. Efforts to shut down the Union Carbide pesticide plant in Institute, West Virginia, and to block the U.S. Department of Energy's plan to locate high-level radioactive waste dumps on Indian reservations, for example, were widely publicized. One possible explanation for this oversight on the part of educational theorists is their tendency to frame social justice issues in terms of the ideals of individual emancipation and economic advancement—which are among the liberal ideas and values they share with the corporate world. And like acrimonious members of a dysfunctional family who often do not recognize what they share in common, liberal educational theorists seem unable to base their thinking on radically different assumptions. To reiterate the point Sale makes, the industrial form of culture that is changing the chemistry of the environment in ways that disproportionately affect minorities and the poor depends on a society of individuals who have been emancipated from the authority of communal traditions and view change as the expression of progress. And since the technological innovations of a science-based industrial culture will be seen as the source of change, science will also be seen as the primary source of progress. Both of these ideas—freeing individuals from the influence of tradition and viewing change in ideas, values, and personal identity as the expression of progress— are also basic aspects of the deep cultural schemata that educational theorists have taken for granted in framing social justice issues. The cultural lenses of these theorists, in effect, enable them to put important issues connected with economic deprivation in focus, but the calibration of the lenses prevents them from recognizing community efforts to reverse the patterns of environmental racism.

It is possible, too, that educational theorists continue to frame the discussion of social justice in ways that exclude environmental issues because they write from a largely urban perspective. For urban dwellers everywhere, the humanly constructed environment of pavement and buildings and the accompanying forms of pollution are a taken-for-granted aspect of daily life. Trees and the occasional open space communicate the same sense of human design that is communicated by the facades of upscale shops and avenues. Food and water are encountered as the end products of a complex infrastructure that also recycles or transports the waste products to outlying areas. In effect, the humanly constructed environment forms the backdrop for the daily conveniences and irritations of city life. Even the artificial nature of the city's many facades of self-sufficiency obscures the complex ecosystems on which its survival depends.

The source of water, the condition of the soil that yields the fruits and vegetables, the ecosystems and human communities displaced or degraded by the technologies that provide the city's energy are out of sight, and thus largely out of mind. Disruptions in the patterns of daily life are seen as the responsibility of city bureaucrats and engineers, and of the business community and labor unions. Without an everyday awareness of the complex relationships between ecosystems and the political economy of transforming Nature into goods and services, the average urban dweller's perception of reality depends largely on images designed to promote consumerism. As office-based work further strengthens the illusions and commodified relationships that are the chief characteristics of urban life, educational theorists readily follow the traditional script and focus on what is corrupt, duplicitous, and exploitative in human relationships. This means framing the social justice mission of education in terms of gender, race, and class. It also means using a postmodern interpretive framework that contrasts sharply with the substantive traditions of the ordinary people who are to be emancipated.

As I later discuss the deep cultural assumptions that leading educational theorists share with the elites they criticize, here I will identify briefly the environmental problems facing the marginalized groups that the radical educational theorists are ignoring. The hazards faced by ethnic minorities and the poor in Detroit are in many ways representative of those found in urban areas across the nation. Paul Mohai and Bunyan Bryant found that the majority of people living closest to commercial hazardous waste facilities (that is, within a one-mile radius) were either members of a minority group or nonminorities living below the poverty line. Following their review of fifteen other studies of the relationship between minority groups, economic status, and environmental hazards (which range from air pollution, exposure to toxins from solid wastes, and toxic fish contamination to the risk of being bitten by rats), Mohai and Bryant concluded that their results and those of the other studies indicate

> both a class and racial bias. Furthermore, that the racial bias is not simply a function of poverty alone also appears to be borne out by the data. All but one of the 11 studies which have examined the distribu-

tion of environmental hazards by race have found a significant bias. In addition, in 5 of the 8 studies where it was possible to assess the relative importance of race with income, racial biases have been found to be more significant. Noteworthy also is the fact that all 3 studies which have been national in scope and which have provided both income and race information have found race to be more importantly related to the distribution of environmental hazards than income. (Mohai and Bunyan 1995:10–23)

In some instances, environmentally hazardous facilities were built before minorities and other low-income families moved into the surrounding neighborhoods. In many others, these groups were deliberately made victims of environmental racism. The indifference of city officials to the fifty-year-long operation of a lead smelter in a predominantly African American west Dallas neighborhood is a case in point. The years of delay that occurred between the discovery that there was a 36 percent increase of lead in the blood level of children and the closing of the smelter would not have been tolerated if the children had been from white, middle-class families. Similar examples of environmental racism can be found throughout the country, with the most extreme cases falling in the corridor stretching from Baton Rouge to New Orleans and along the Texas border with Mexico.

If the creation of social and material wealth at the community level is one of the responsibilities of an eco-justice pedagogy, understanding the forms of environmental contamination and the political processes necessary for eliminating them should be equally important. An eco-justice pedagogy that addresses these issues will have a more immediate influence on the quality of daily life than a pedagogy that denounces "white terror" and teaches the language of emancipation, which colonizes even as it pretends to decolonize. There are additional dimensions of an eco-justice pedagogy that need to be taken into account. The following guidelines will help theorists avoid the contradictions inherent in the progressive vision of social justice that now characterizes current thinking about educational reform.

1. An eco-justice pedagogy must be based on a recognition of the fundamental differences between high- and low-status forms of knowledge and the value systems that accompany them. The current distinction is one that universities created as interpreters and custodians of the Enlightenment vision of a rationally ordered world. They continue to maintain it through their increasingly close collaboration with corporations and government in the creation of new technologies and expert systems. None of the educational metaphors used to legitimize the autonomous, rational, self-directed individual that is supposed to result from a university education have any connection with the personal attributes necessary for participation in the kind of community that Sale describes. As the metaphors encode the ideals envisioned by Western political philosophers as a universal moral framework, it is difficult to criticize them—especially if one takes for granted the modern form of consciousness and ignores how it is contributing to environmental degradation. As the high-status knowledge of universities converges with the symbolic skills needed by corporations, the legitimizing metaphors are beginning to sound dated—although that has not diminished their use within conservative, liberal, and even radical circles. The list of metaphors includes *individual freedom, empowerment, critical reflection, progress,* and *democracy* (the latter is always understood as advancing individual freedom and a progressive form of change). If we can keep a sense of distance from the god-word status of these metaphors, it becomes easier to recognize that they do not represent the knowledge, skills, and values associated with membership in the kind of interdependent community Sale describes. These metaphors, along with those used by radical edu-

cators (e.g., *resistance, difference, critical pedagogy, predatory culture,* and *revolutionary multiculturalism*), frame the purpose of education in terms of emancipating the individual from all forms of communal authority and responsibility. Generally unrecognized is how both groups of educational metaphors reflect an idealized image of individualism that fits more the needs of a market-dominated culture than the view of community held by Gandhi, Wendell Berry, and the Luddites. It is also important to recognize that these metaphors do not lead to forms of individualism that would be at home in the majority of the world's cultures. Ironically, this Western type of individual can be found in every part of the world playing the role of salesperson for a multinational corporation, engineer, or scientist collecting patentable genetic material.

To summarize the main point: the knowledge, skills, and patterns of social interaction that contribute to participation in intergenerationally connected and morally responsible communities are not learned in public school and university classrooms. In short, the ideal promoted by the educational and corporate world is the individual who possesses the ability to live anywhere, solve problems in ways that integrate technologies into a worldwide system, and keep pace with the learning curve set by the need for new technologies and markets.

2. An eco-justice pedagogy requires shifting from a global perspective to one that recognizes the multiplicity of cultures. One of the characteristics of high-status knowledge that perpetuates the decontextualized thinking of Western philosophers and social theorists is thinking in terms of universals. As Alvin Gouldner describes it: "Its ideal is: 'one word, one meaning,' for everyone and forever" (1979:28). Metaphors such as *democracy, development, justice,* and *individual freedom* encode a long history of Western experiences and rational debate. In spite of their cultural rootedness, they have been treated as representing universal aspirations—even for

cultures that are not based on Western assumptions and values. In *Grassroots Post-modernism: Remaking the Soil of Cultures* (1998), Gustavo Esteva and Madhu Suri Prakash argue that making the Western ideal of human rights the universal yardstick for the world's cultures is itself an expression of cultural "recolonization" (110–146). In their view, the Western legal system, which is often represented as protecting the rights of the individual, destroys the capacity of local cultures to resolve problems through their own networks of mutual support. Many of their examples of how human rights activists disrupt the capacity of indigenous cultures to rely on their long-standing traditions for dealing with individuals and groups that violate the moral norms of the community are convincing, yet their arguments appear one-sided and thus overly simplistic. While claiming not to be moral relativists, they nevertheless take the position that injustices are best handled according to the local customs of the community. And in many instances, what Westerners perceive as injustice may not violate the moral norms and patterns of local communities.

Esteva and Prakash's arguments for recognizing the resourcefulness of indigenous cultures and the destructive results of Western efforts to impose various universal systems on them need to be considered in any formulation of an eco-justice pedagogy. Some cultural practices not mentioned in their book, such as female circumcision; killing of young women to restore family honor, or *sharaf* (a centuries-old tradition in some Islamic cultures); exploitation of child labor; caste systems; and sectarian-based violence also need to be considered. The Taliban law preventing Afghan women from working outside the household and from pursuing an education is a particularly tragic violation of what Western cultures regard as basic human rights. As religious custom also prevents male physicians from treating female patients, the women of Afghanistan no longer have access to medical treatment. In effect, the arguments in *Grassroots Post-modernism* misrepresent the complexity that surrounds the problem of reform by focusing on indigenous cultures (such as the Indian people of Oaxaca and such renowned cultural figures as Gandhi) that have successfully managed their own moral and social ecologies. Nevertheless, this book, along with others such as *The Development Dictionary: A Guide to Knowledge as Powers,* edited by Wolfgang Sachs (1992), and Frédérique Apffel-Marglin's *Spirit of Regeneration: Andean Culture Confronting Western Notions of Development* (1998) that highlight cultural differences in the individual's relationship to the larger community, are especially important to avoiding formulaic and messianic forms of progressive thinking that would make schools sites for developing an individual-centered egalitarian society. Literature written from an indigenous perspective puts into focus the destructive consequences that often arise from imposing universal prescriptions on other cultures such as the need for a global economy, universal human rights, individual freedom, the Information Age, and a Western form of higher education. Indigenous literature also describes the varied ways in which local cultures have adapted to the limits and possibilities of their ecosystems and have developed complex symbolic systems that sustain communal patterns of interdependence in work, entertainment, healing, and ceremonies. But most important, this literature brings out the many forms of cultural intelligence that have developed as alternatives to a consumer- and technology-dependent form of culture. These different forms of cultural intelligence, expressed in the traditions and practices of moral reciprocity of such diverse groups as the Hopi, Latinos, and the Amish, can be understood only from an insider's perspective. Without this in-depth understanding, an eco-justice pedagogy will become simply another form of cultural imposition—even as it proclaims itself to be in the service of emancipatory ideals. The use of cultural lenses that highlight examples of race, class, and gender abuses is as problematic as the use of cultural lenses that highlight only the positive attributes of a cultural group.

The shift in focus from the abstract and universal to a careful consideration of local cultural patterns needs a reference point that is not grounded in the shifting sands of cultural relativism. This grounding, as I have suggested elsewhere, lies in the assessment of the impact that indigenous cultures have on the ecosystems on which they and future generations depend. Whether cultural practices lead to living within the sustaining capacity of local ecosystems or result in degrading the local environment as well as that of other cultural groups becomes critical to the curricular content of an eco-justice pedagogy. Whether the cultural patterns support morally coherent communities or create distortions that privilege certain groups over others is also an important consideration.

In effect, an eco-justice pedagogy that accepts the ability of minority cultures to renew and even revise their traditions in light of internal and external changes cannot avoid continually reformulating itself. However, this does not mean that it should serve the interests of local elites or ignore forms of dehumanization that may be accepted within a particular culture. There is still a need for advocates of human rights, just as there is a need for an educational process that promotes deep cultural transformation. An eco-justice pedagogy should avoid the sense of certainty that comes with the reification of Western ideas and values—particularly those that co-evolved with the Industrial Revolution—and balance the insider's cultural traditions with what is understood about environmental and intercultural changes that represent destructive worldwide trends.

3. An eco-justice pedagogy must distinguish between the deep cultural assumptions underlying the last hundred years of emancipatory theories of education in North America and those on

which minority cultures and the non-Western cultures that comprise the majority of the world's population are based. Key Western assumptions about the progressive nature of change, the individual being the basic social unit, the ability of critical reflection to establish what has conceptual and moral authority, and the corresponding rejection of tradition as an oppressive impediment to progress are noticeably absent from the ways of thinking of the oldest and most populated cultures in the non-Western world.

Esteva and Prakash state this basic difference between Western and non-Western cultures in the following way: "For the 'social minorities,' the vast chasm that separates organic from industrial memory is not sensed. In their other worlds, still separate from the monoculture of modernity, the 'social majorities' depend only on organic memory. Like their dead, they have escaped the growing dependence of the 'social minorities' on industrial memory" (1998:67). "Organic memories" encompass the narratives, ceremonies, customs, and practices of moral reciprocity, everyday patterns reinforced through face-to-face relationships. Like the cells of an organism, these traditions are continually renewed—with change reflecting the communal response to internal and external processes.

The tension between organic memory and industrial memory (which erases the past in order to focus on future progress) is brought out even more clearly in the following observation by Gerald Berthoud:

> Development, beyond the obvious need to produce ever more goods and services, is a process through which must emerge a new kind of human being and corresponding institutions. What must be universalized through development is a cultural complex centered around the notion that human life, if it is to be fully lived, cannot be constrained by limits of any kind. To produce such a result in traditional societies, for whom the supposedly primordial principle of boundless expan-

sion in the technological and economic domains is generally alien, presupposed overcoming symbolic and moral "obstacles," that is, ridding these societies of various inhibiting ideas and practices such as myths, ceremonies, rituals, mutual aid, networks of solidarity, and the like. (1992:72)

In short, the traditions of the community must be eliminated, with the modern "antitradition traditions" becoming the basis of a society of consumer-dependent individuals.

Stated in the contemporary political vocabulary, an eco-justice pedagogy must combine a responsibility for contributing to social justice (in the domains of both culture and natural ecology) while at the same time helping to conserve traditions essential to communities that retain the mutuality and moral reciprocity of the commons. Conserving living traditions does not mean maintaining the status quo, nor does it involve supporting reactionary interests. But it may involve helping regenerate traditions of noncommodified relationships and skills that have been largely marginalized by the modern forces of production and consumption—and by the forms of knowledge promoted in public schools and universities. The task of conserving what contributes to the recovery of the ecological and cultural commons, in turn, requires an understanding of local interests, needs, and traditions. This understanding needs to be framed within the larger context of worldwide ecological trends such as global warming and the toxic contamination of the environment.

Many competing theories address educational reform. In order to understand the fundamental difference between an eco-justice pedagogy based on a deep cultural and ecological way of thinking and theories of educational reform still based on the assumptions that underlie modern culture, it is necessary to examine the latter in some depth. The tendency of current educational theorists to represent Dewey as providing a conceptual framework for addressing the educational aspects of the environmental crisis serves as an example of the conceptual confusion that continues to exist. Making minor modifications in a theoretical framework in order to accommodate newly recognized issues and challenges too often means giving lip-service to their importance while carrying on the educational practices that contributed to the problem in the first place. The following chapters clarify why an eco-justice pedagogy needs to be based on a radical reconceptualization of basic assumptions rather than on the assimilation of an eco-justice vocabulary into existing progressive theories of educational reform. They also explain why the most popular theorists of educational reform are unable to articulate the role of education in reestablishing the balance between cultural practices and the regenerating capacity of natural systems.

Chapter 1 examines how the contradictions and silences in progressive theories of education lead to an assimilation approach to social justice issues. The theories of John Dewey and Paulo Freire are still considered as providing curricular and pedagogical guidelines for ameliorating the causes of the inequality and oppression faced by marginalized groups. Thus, any serious approach to rectifying the conceptual and moral foundations of an eco-justice pedagogy must begin with an analysis of their theories. A second major focus of the chapter is on the more contemporary educational theorists who have synthesized the ideas of Dewey, Freire, Marx, and the Frankfurt School of Critical Sociology. Their writings on race, class, gender, and multiculturalism are viewed by many of the more socially conscious professors of education as providing the essential guidelines for using the classroom to reform American society. The position that Peter McLaren shares with other "radical" educational theorists, whom he calls "progressive left-liberal multiculturalists," suggests a growing awareness that differences in cultures need to be taken into account in both the analysis of how schools contribute to cultural domination and in prescriptions for social reform. The use of a "progressive left-liberal" set of assumptions as the basis for understanding non-Western cultural groups is symptomatic, however, of the double binds in their writings that continue to go unrecognized.

Chapter 2 focuses on educational theories that are based on extrapolations from recent developments in science. The basic question that frames the analysis is: Can science provide the conceptual and moral framework for an eco-justice pedagogy? Educational theorists are attempting to turn recent developments in the physical and biological sciences into full-blown social theories that can be used to guide educational reform. Developments in the field of neuroscience, for example, are being translated into a series of recommendations for matching curricular and pedagogical practices with stages of brain development. This area of scientific research has particularly important implications that may set back by decades recent educational gains in achieving a more equitable society.

Some educational theorists view the physical sciences as engaged in a paradigm shift that has immense implications for how we think about education. Systems theory and the complexity sciences provide a different way of understanding natural processes—one that recognizes the self-organizing characteristics of open, nonlinear systems. While it is understandable that educational theorists would urge the abandonment of educational practices based on the mechanistic model derived from Newtonian science, the "process" approach to education now being interpreted as consistent with the characteristics of dissipative structures raises serious questions.

The "science envy" that characterizes the thinking of several educational theorists has other disturbing implications that need to be considered in the context of an eco-justice pedagogy. Borrowing from science a conceptual and moral framework for reforming education opens the door for the reemergence of the racist thinking that was part of the legacy of nineteenth-century science. The new metanarrative being constructed by proponents of evolutionary biology such as Richard Dawkins, E. O. Wilson, and Daniel C. Dennett is having an impact on many academic disciplines. It is only a matter of time before educational theorists who view science as the primary source of intellectual authority come under the influence of evolutionary theory. Their challenge will be to reconcile liberal values with the theory that explains how better-adapted individuals and cultural groups are more likely to pass on their genes and cultural patterns.

Chapter 3 addresses the arguments that making computers available in classrooms on a more equitable basis will help rectify the causes of social inequality. Computer literacy, in this view, is essential both to entrance into the workforce and to equal citizenship in the emerging global culture of cyberspace. These arguments are compelling, but they do not take account of the culture-mediating characteristics of computer technology. Chapter 3 examines two fundamental sets of relationships ignored by those who advocate preparing students to participate in the digital culture. The first has to do with the connections between the cultural patterns of thought, values, and community reinforced by the mediating characteristics of computers and the ecological crisis. The connections between computers and economic globalization are generally recognized, but the proclivity to think of computers as the latest expression of progress has prevented computer advocates from recognizing that computers reinforce the very cultural patterns that have a long history of exploiting and degrading the environment.

The second set of fundamental relationships relates to how computer-mediated thought and communication undermine cultural diversity. The often amazing capabilities of computers have diverted attention from the many forms of cultural knowledge that they cannot communicate. These marginalized cultural patterns—mythopoetic narratives that are the basis of a cultural group's moral codes, systems of intergenerational communication and responsibility, face-to-face activities that represent alternatives to monetized relationships, and so forth—are basic to the self-identity of many cultural groups in North America. The eco-justice implications of losing these forms of knowledge and interdependencies are thus the main focus of this chapter.

Chapter 4 identifies the main themes of an eco-justice curriculum that are essential to democratize decisions that are now being made by experts who have been educated to link cultural convergence with progress. Themes such as the nature of commodification, tradition, technology, science, and language can be introduced in the early grades and examined in later grades in relation to different ideologies and cultural traditions. The chapter also addresses how these themes enable students to address eco-justice issues in their own communities. I argue that students should learn about how the deep assumptions of different cultural groups in North America lead to different interpretations of the themes that should be at the core of an eco-justice curriculum. This chapter thus clarifies one of the fundamental differences between an eco-justice pedagogy and the reform proposals that uphold different modes of inquiry but never specify which aspects of the dominant and minority cultures should be included in the curriculum.

Chapter 5 addresses the need for consistency between pedagogy and curriculum in a culturally diverse and ecologically problematic world and examines the differences between an eco-justice pedagogy and the pedagogy advocated by educational theorists following in the footsteps of John Dewey, Paulo Freire, Alfred North Whitehead, and Ilya Prigogine. The teacher's mediating role in the process of primary socialization—which requires a deep understanding of the connections between a cultural way of knowing, language, and communicative competence—is also given extended consideration. The way primary socialization is carried out has lasting effects on students' ability to make implicit cultural patterns explicit, and thus to recognize how thought and behavior reproduce earlier forms of thinking passed along through the metaphorical constructions in the language of the curriculum. Finally, I consider the importance of an eco-justice pedagogy being based on an understanding of cultural differences in metacommunication. The teacher must understand the nature of primary socialization in a culturally diverse classroom and the miscommunication that results when cultural differences in metacommunication patterns are not understood if the core themes of an eco-justice curriculum are to become an empowering educational experience.

1 Emancipatory Theories of Education

The Enlightenment vision of societies based on reason and on the progressive emancipation of individuals, as interpreted by modern American educational theorists, continues to ignore the destructive impact that the tools of rationality have had on the environment. Nature writers such as Henry David Thoreau, John Muir, and Richard Jeffries questioned the ravaged condition of the industrial landscape, but their writings failed to slow the juggernaut of industrial development and the spread of consumerism. Indeed, it was not until the appearance of Aldo Leopold's *A Sand County Almanac* (1947) and Rachel Carson's *Silent Spring* (1962) that an awareness of the need for a land ethic began to inch its way into the public consciousness. Ironically, many indigenous cultures that did not share the assumptions of past and present Enlightenment thinkers had already encoded a land ethic into their ceremonies, technologies, and patterns of community life well before European adventurers arrived in search of riches. The assumptions underlying Enlightenment thinking shaped language, and thus thought processes, in ways that prevented earlier generations of

Americans from learning from indigenous cultures—even though these cultures possessed important knowledge of local natural systems. These same assumptions are also reproduced in the language now used to legitimate the current process of cultural colonization popularly known as "globalization."

Given the use of the Enlightenment view of rationality to exploit nature and to categorize other cultural ways of knowing as backward and irrational, two questions become paramount. First, do the theories of John Dewey, Paulo Freire, Peter McLaren, Henry Giroux, Michael Apple, and others who view themselves in the emancipatory tradition of educational thought utilize a post-Enlightenment language that avoids the problems of cultural colonization and anthropocentrism that have been a central feature of Western Enlightenment thinking? Second, do these theories recognize the noncommodified characteristics of community life that are shared in urban and rural settings, and by cultures based on profoundly different mythopoetic narratives? These questions open doors that Western elites have wedged shut for hundreds of years—conceptual doors connected with pathways of development that are not centered on turning communities into market-governed relationships.

The question that needs to be asked of contemporary emancipatory educational theorists is whether their concern for cultural differences is articulated in a language that encodes the deep assumptions of the Enlightenment—assumptions about the linear nature of change (which is equated with progress), the power of critical reflection to emancipate individuals from the hold of tradition, the "invisible hand" that underlies the rules governing legitimate discourse (the marketplace of ideas), the oppressive nature of communal patterns of solidarity, and the anthropocentric view of human-Nature relationships. There is also the question of whether their language frames cultural differences in ways that continue to privilege the authority of these Enlightenment assumptions. Finally, we must ask whether the educational process they represent as leading to a more emancipated form of individualism will result in the loss of cultural knowledge of how to live within the limits and possibility of the natural environment. This latter concern must be kept in the forefront of any discussion of how emancipatory theorists explain the nature of oppression within other cultural groups and the form of subjectivity and lifestyle they want to see adopted.

In arguing that emancipatory educational theorists rely on a metaphorical language that encodes deep, culturally specific assumptions that are part of the legacy of the Western Enlightenment, I am not at the same time assuming that every culture's approach to social justice is equally valid. That is, I do not want to see a doctrine of cultural relativism substituted for basic human rights that must be universally respected. Furthermore, in framing the discussion of how emancipatory theorists' fixation on issues of class, race, and gender obscures the more complex and daunting challenges of an eco-justice pedagogy, I am not ignoring the systemic inequalities and abuses present in the dominant, high-status culture. On many social justice issues I am in full agreement with them—particularly on social justice issues related to gender, minority cultures, and the economic underclass. Indeed, I want to expand the list of injustices to include the right of future generations to experience life in an uncontaminated environment, the need for cultures to sustain patterns of moral reciprocity along with knowledge and activities that result in a more ecologically sustainable footprint, and the need for more ecologically centered cultural groups to assess which technological and linguistic innovations can be assimilated and which must be rejected.

A further qualification needs to be made before we proceed to an examination of the double binds in the language of emancipatory educational theorists. While the cultures I focus on here have developed patterns of community that are well attuned to the perturbations and cycles of local environments, I am also aware that some cultures have had a destructive impact. I am aware, too, of cultures that have developed complex ways of understanding how to successfully utilize the biodiversity of their environment while also engaging in horrendous forms of gender and social class discrimination and child abuse. Thus, the analysis cannot be reduced to the oppositional categories of progressive versus oppressive cultures, ecologically destructive versus ecologically benign patterns, radical progressivism versus reactionary conservatism, and, to use the language of the educational theorists, emancipatory versus the banking approach to education that does not allow for critical reflection.

If we return to Kirkpatrick Sale's description of the aspects of community that had to be overturned in order for the industrial mode of production and consumption to emerge as a revolutionary force in the late eighteenth and early nineteenth centuries, we can obtain a clearer understanding of how the thinking of the emancipatory educational theorists, if fully implemented in public schools, would not fundamentally alter the course of development that the Luddites were revolting against. In fact, these educators' prescriptions, while cloaked in an anticapitalist and social justice rhetoric, would further undermine cultures that have managed to retain the patterns of community self-sufficiency that represent an alternative to the industrial model of existence. According to Sale, three traditions had to be subverted in order to implement the form of individualism required by the industrial process: self-sufficiency, mutual aid, and morality in the marketplace. Self-sufficiency of the community requires a combination of knowledge and skill in the production of food, clothing, and household and community necessities. Self-sufficiency also applies to the ability of the community to participate in decision making about the use of common resources. Furthermore, it requires that the present generation's means of attaining self-sufficiency should not diminish the capacity of future generations to attain the same level of existence.

Mutual aid has many dimensions that are integral to self-sufficient communities—including interpersonal relationships regulated by an awareness of the moral imperative to respond to the needs of others. The individual and community patterns of moral reciprocity also extend to human-Nature relationships. Mutual aid is also expressed in the intergenerational sharing of communal knowledge, ceremonies, and the use of technologies. Mentoring is an expression of mutual aid. So is the sharing of elder knowledge that helps avoid mistakes that come from a lack of experience and short-range perspective.

Morality in the marketplace involves the recognition that market relationships, while a necessary part of community life, are not the primary basis of human interactions and values. Viewed cross-culturally, it is expressed in how the mythopoetic narratives of cultural groups provide the moral templates that govern human and human-Nature relationships. Cultures that represent humans and nonhuman life forms as parts of a single, interdependent process of creation are governed by moral frameworks that severely limit market relationships. Even in the dominant Western culture in which morality in the marketplace has become largely an economic decision, there are still some aspects of human life that cannot be patented, manufactured, and sold without encountering resistance from cultural groups that cling to preindustrial values. Perhaps the most important expression of morality in the marketplace involves limiting the introduction of technologies that create dehumanizing working conditions or lead to lost work opportunities. As Sale points out, the Luddites saw their highly skilled approach to the use of technology, which was integrated into the life of the community, being replaced by technologies that reduced work to a mechanistic process and made irrelevant those skills and community values that did not fit the new logic of equating greater efficiency with increased profits. Their attacks on the factories of Manchester and other Midland towns were as much a protest against the destruction of their communities as a protest against the radically new technology and the system for organizing it. This is a point that the critics of the Luddites usually fail to recognize.

Additional patterns of traditional community life that Sale cites as impeding the creation of the consumer-dependent individual include "stubborn tradition, regulation by custom, [and] organic knowledge instead of mechanistic science." As the writings of emancipatory theorists from Dewey and Freire to McLaren and Giroux are based on the Enlightenment view of tradition, customs, and local knowledge of natural phenomena, it is necessary to provide a more expanded explanation of these aspects of community life. Sale's phrase "stubborn tradition" is the one that evokes the most extreme reaction from these educational theorists. As the nature of tradition is both the most widely misunderstood and yet the most complex aspect of human experience, I shall discuss it first.

Enlightenment thinkers associated the word *tradition* with the legacy of a feudal social order that limited human choice and personal development, the wealth and privileges of the church and aristocracy, superstitions that swept over communities like a life-destroying distemper, and a political process that was not accountable to the impoverished and increasingly exploited masses. Social relations based on rational thought were seen as the necessary antidote for the many ills associated with tradition. René Descartes and John Locke, in particular, contributed to the association of tradition with all that is limiting and socially unjust by explaining in very different ways that the source of ideas is not tradition but rather the operations of the rational mind and direct experience.

Locke exerted an even more lasting influence on how tradition has been understood by explaining how language serves as a conduit for communicating ideas that arise through the direct experience of individuals. Locke did not understand the metaphorical nature of language (the Aristotelian view of metaphor continued to be deeply entrenched in educated circles until the 1950s) or the nature of culture. Without an understanding of the complex symbolic basis of cultural experience, including how culture is encoded and carried forward and its largely taken-for-granted status in daily experience, it is impossible to fully understand the nature of tradition. The two men's limited understanding of tradition further restricted their ability to recognize that the rational process and the experiential basis of ideas were themselves expressions of a debate within a specific cultural way of knowing. Following in the tradition of Western philosophy, they based their epistemologies on the assumption that the individual is the basic social unit that engages in rational thought and has direct, culturally unmediated experiences. Thus, tradition, from their perspective, was an impediment to the rational self-determination of the individual—a way of thinking still espoused by emancipatory educational theorists and other modern thinkers.

A strong case can be made that the authority of tradition in people's lives (which, as Hannah Arendt points out, is profoundly different from the authoritarianism of external control) had to be overturned at an ideological level as part of the convergence of cultural changes that promoted the modernizing process. In effect, while people continued to act and think in traditional patterns, they had to be indoctrinated to equate tradition with backwardness. In order to create the new myth (metanarrative) that equates every sort of change—from experiments introduced into culture by "advances" in scientific knowledge to the relentless pursuit of new ideas and values by supposedly autonomous individuals—it was necessary to represent tradition in increasingly distorted and simplistic terms. If people could be made to believe that they could live fuller, happier lives when freed from the constraints of traditions, they would be less likely to resist basing their lives on increasingly experimental and life-shaping technological innovations. Today, the connection between institutions furthering the digital phase of the Industrial Revolution and the systematic misrepresentation that equates tradition with backwardness and oppression can be seen in the popular distinction between "modern" and "traditional" cultures. This same distinction, with its bias in favor of consumer-oriented, technologically dependent, individual-centered cultures, can also be seen in the connotations associated with "developed" and "undeveloped" cultures.

The process of industrialization is now being extended to the basic biological processes that sustain all forms of life. Not only can everything now be treated as a commodity that can be manufactured, but the basic characteristics of the person can be engineered to requirements of the marketplace. This "everything is for sale" ethos has also required a change to a consciousness free of the influence of traditional values and ways of thinking that foreground the reciprocal nature of communal relationships and responsibilities. Susan Bordo's *The Flight to Objectivity: Essays on Cartesianism and Culture* (1987), Vandana Shiva's *Monocultures of the Mind: Biodiversity, Biotechnology, and the Third World* (1993), and Andrew Kimbrell's *The Human Body Shop: The Engineering and Marketing of Life* (1993) are just a small part of the current literature that exposes how the traditions of industrial culture advance by destroying traditions that represent alternative moral practices and noncommodified relationships.

The phrase "traditions of industrial culture" provides a starting point for a more general discussion of the nature of tradition. Again, I must remind readers that the following discussion is not an argument for embracing *all* traditions; nor is it an argument for tradition itself—as if modernization could be carried to the extreme where all traditions would disappear. While the emancipatory educational theorists advocate numerous "antitradition traditions," including a form of existence involving continual change based on the critical reflection of the individual, I will be more explicit about the need to renew traditions that contribute to morally coherent, noncommodified communities that have an ecologically sustainable footprint.

Nearly every aspect of industrial culture, from scientific knowledge and technological innovations to the mode of inquiry and forms of high-status knowledge promoted in our universities, is actually based on traditions that were handed down from the past and continue to undergo continual modification. Many aspects of industrial culture, particularly those activities, ideas, and products that have a short survival time of only seconds, days, months, or even a year, should be understood as fads or momentary fashions. That is, they do not last long enough to become new traditions—though the patterns of thought, values, and technological practices that gave them their mode of expression may continue on as traditions. Similarly, many of the ideas and metaphorical images used by the emancipatory educators are not likely to be passed from generation to generation, but the deep root metaphors that organize the ideas into culturally predictable patterns of thinking, and even the subject-verb-object pattern used to express them, nevertheless represent traditions that go far back in time.

A full account of the nature of tradition would require an accounting of all the practices, patterns of interaction, foods, ceremonies, technologies, and material forms of expression handed down from the past to the present. For the dominant culture, a more specific list would include the use of money, systems for organizing work, legal procedures, ways of viewing youth and older people, reification of the ideal body type for women and men, patterns of discrimination, moral values, the authority of print-based communication, perspectivism in art, and the layout of communities. The word *tradition* is thus as broad in meaning as the word *culture.* In fact, *tradition* is the word that best refers to the continuities that connect current forms of cultural expression to the past. The key point that Edward Shils makes in his exhaustive analysis of the complexity of tradition is that it is impossible to live without re-enacting and, over time, modifying traditions. As I said earlier, suggesting that individuals can be emancipated from traditions is like suggesting that they can be emancipated from their embeddedness in the symbolic and technological systems we call culture.

Shils also recommends that the most accurate way to understand tradition is to think of it as being organic—like a plant with branches that are in various states of growth and decay and with largely unseen roots extending to various depths that also include the mix of the new and the no longer vital. To change the metaphor slightly, traditions should be viewed as changing slowly, with some changes being slower than the majority of people desire while other traditions, such as privacy, craft knowledge, and noncommodified relationships, are changing faster and even disappearing before people are aware of their loss. On the other hand, some traditions that are still vital should not have been constituted in the first place. These include racism, sexism, and treating the environment as a resource to be exploited as quickly as possible. Any practice that survives over the time span of four cohorts, according to Shils, must be considered a tradition. That is, the practice has to be passed on over four generations before people lose sight of its origins (and thus its relative status) and adopt a taken-for-granted attitude toward it. Since a tradition cannot be recovered after it has been entirely lost, it is imperative that people understand which traditions are essential to communities that live in harmony with themselves and their environment. The difficulty of recovering traditions is evident in the Disney theme parks that attempt to replicate the traditions of wildness but succeed only in strengthening the traditions of commodification. And the way important traditions can be undermined without public debate can be seen in the ubiquitous use of computer-based monitoring technologies that now collect data on every aspect of what once was considered our private lives.

Sale's reference to "stubborn tradition" takes on an entirely different meaning when tradition is understood in this more complex way. The Luddites were stubborn to the point of armed rebellion because they saw the industrial process, and the values on which it was based, as threatening their community-centered traditions. As they had not yet been socialized to the myth that equates change with linear progress, they resisted the social experiment being imposed on them by scientists, industrialists, and the liberal thinkers who were laying the conceptual groundwork for the modern state and the autonomous individual. An example of "stubborn tradition" in contemporary American life is feminists' efforts to change traditions that cannot be reconciled with other traditional values and ideas—such as equality and the right of individual reproductive choice. Ethnic groups have been able to retain their distinct identities only by holding stubbornly to their traditions—even as these have been modified by modern traditions. That Shils is correct in saying that traditions are not static and that they do not carry themselves forward independent of human behavior can be seen in the accommodations that traditionally oriented cultural groups have made with modern technologies and values. For example, the Kachinas still hold their ceremonial dances on the mesas of northern Arizona, but much of the food and gifts distributed as part of the ceremony has been purchased at the local supermarket. The satirical skits enacted between different phases of the ceremony draw on themes in modern life. Another example can be found in the traditional foods still prepared by Latino, Asian American, and Jewish families. Even though modern technologies and values have led to minor and even major changes in these traditions, they are still the basis of an intergenerational experience and identity.

Sale's reference to the need to subvert the tradition of "organic . . . science" in order for the new type of individual to emerge is also important to clarifying the connections between the assumptions that underlie emancipatory educators' interpretation of social justice and certain ideas and values that coevolved with the Industrial Revolution. Organic science is a cumulative body of knowledge acquired over generations of direct experience and hypothesis testing within a bioregion—knowledge that often makes the difference between an adequate diet and starvation. Because of its intergenerational nature, organic science is interwoven with the cultural group's understanding of interdependent relationships— which makes it part of the group's moral code. Examples of organic science in agriculture abound. Northern Indian women, for example, know how to use 150 different species of plants for vegetables, fodder, and health care. Peasants near Veracruz, Mexico, utilize 435 wild plants and animal species for a variety of purposes. It was organic science created by centuries of observation that enabled the indigenous people of the Andes to grow more than 3,500 varieties of potatoes and 1,500 varieties of quinoa. The practice of intercropping, used by indigenous cultures around the world, is yet another example of organic science. Those of us socialized to the claims of mechanistic/industrial science are particularly astonished by indigenous people's knowledge of edible plants and their ability to utilize wild plants and animals without destroying the organisms' capacity to regenerate. Mechanistic science has undermined the ability of communities to pass the knowledge of their bioregion on to the next generation. At the same time that the emergent ideology of liberalism was exhorting individuals to free themselves from the constraints of traditional knowledge, mechanistic science has been narrowing the gene pool while promoting genetically engineered plants that require fertilizers, pesticides, heavy machinery, and the yearly purchase of seed stock.

Unlike organic science, mechanistic science is analytical, reductionist, and dependent on a literacy form of consciousness that marginalizes the importance of local contexts (including local knowledge derived from intergenerational experience). It is mathematically oriented in ways that lead to easy integration into the value system of the industrial model of production. Additional qualities that differentiate it from organic science include its secularizing orientation and its presumption to being a culture-free mode of observation and hypothesis testing. The history of mechanistic science is the history of industrial agriculture, the industrialization of the household and community, and, now, the industrialization of the reproductive process in plants, animals, and humans.

The distinction between organic and mechanistic science may seem totally irrelevant to how emancipatory educators frame the discussion of social justice in American society. But a careful examination of the differences between the two brings out three critical points that are marginalized by the language of emancipation. First is the importance of cultural diversity in an ecologically uncertain world. This is brought out in the following observation by Stephen A. Marglin:

> If the only certainty about the future is that the future is uncertain, if the only sure thing is that we are in for surprises, then no amount of planning, no amount of prescription, can deal with the contingencies that the future will reveal. That is why ultimately there can be no agriculture for the people that is not agriculture of the people, agriculture by the people.
>
> People's knowledge developed over centuries, even millennia, is the most important safeguard against disaster and the most sure basis of a resilient, adaptive agriculture.
>
> For this reason, diversity is as necessary to development as human

beings as it is to ecological balance. Diversity may indeed be the key to the survival of the human species.... But within the human species culture rather than instinct bears the primary load of the intergenerational transmission of knowledge. (1996:241)

This point is also echoed in the writings of Vandana Shiva, Wes Jackson, and Frédérique Apffel-Marglin.

Second, organic knowledge of the nutritional and healing properties of wild plants, which is now becoming the object of what Shiva calls "biopiracy," weaves together tradition, intergenerational responsibility, mutuality within the community, and a clear understanding of human dependency on ecosystems that are subject to rapid and unpredictable changes. As many other traditions are essential to socially just and ecologically viable communities, the question becomes: Does the language of the emancipatory educational theorists provide a basis for distinguishing between destructive traditions and those that are beneficial?

The third issue brought out by an understanding of the characteristics of organic science needs to be framed in terms of the language of contemporary political ideologies. As a careful examination of emancipatory educators' use of political categories will show, *conservatism* is used to designate what they consider to be reactionary, as the justification for the economically and politically privileged class, and is associated with apologists for the Western mode of production. However, if we focus specifically on determining whether organic science is actually the expression of a form of cultural/bio-conservatism and whether mechanistic science is closer to the values and assumptions of progressive or even radical liberalism, we can see a double bind emerging. These educators criticize mechanistic science and the industrial system and would likely agree that organic science, in spite of its intergenerational nature (which they would be quite uncomfortable with), is more democratic than the forms of social organization connected with the history of mechanistic science. But would they be able to acknowledge that their language marginalizes the importance of communal and intergenerational patterns that are essential features of organic science?

A study of the genealogy of their emancipatory language will show that it goes back to the philosophers and political theorists who viewed mechanistic science as a powerful metaphor for the organization of vernacular cultures into the nation-state and for the development of strategies to emancipate individuals from communal traditions. As I show in the following analysis, emancipatory educational theorists use *culture* and other context-free metaphors in a way that enables them to avoid acknowledging the double binds that characterize their writings on social justice.

Peter McLaren and Henry Giroux

I begin the analysis with the ideas of Peter McLaren and Henry Giroux, the most visible spokespersons on the relationship between an emancipatory pedagogy and the achievement of social justice. The complexity of McLaren's analysis and the range of issues mentioned but not explored in his writings provide a useful starting point for assessing whether the emancipatory way of framing social justice issues is a complex word game being played by tenured academicians or the basis of an eco-justice pedagogy. McLaren continually denounces every possible expression of elitism, but he does it using a vocabulary that makes little or no sense to the person on the street, classroom teachers, or the various ethnic groups he seeks to rescue from oppression. McLaren's audience is thus necessarily limited to the small group of educational and neo-Marxist theorists who share the theoretical tradition promoted in many graduate schools—the primary training grounds for today's elites.

His highly abstract vocabulary raises the question of whom it is intended to motivate: other theorists who think in the same decontextualized language, or the cultural groups that still retain, in spite of the complex and subtle assimilation pressures, ways of thinking that diverge from the deep assumptions that underlie McLaren's thinking. There is also the question of whether his emphasis on the need for continual critical analysis (like continual revolution) can be translated into concrete pedagogical and curricular recommendations. The following is typical of the level of abstraction that characterizes his recommendations. In the chapter titled "White Terror and Oppositional Agency: Toward a Critical Multiculturalism," he writes: "We need to occupy locations between our political unconsciousness and everyday praxis but at the same time be guided by a universal emancipatory world view in the form of a provisional utopia or contingent foundationalism" (1995:141). Another recommendation is framed in the same context-free language of continual emancipation: "If we are to be redeemed from our finitude as passive suppliants of history, we must, as students and teachers, adopt more oppositional and politically combative social and cultural practices" (143–144). When no specific traditions of any culture are affirmed as worthy of being part of the student's learning experience except as an object of "oppositional and politically combative" classroom analysis, one can only wonder if McLaren understands the difference between emancipation and nihilism.

There are instances when the wheel of theory seems finally about to touch the ground of everyday reality, such as when McLaren refers to the "cyber-nomads," or, in a more recent article, to the problem of social justice in the age of globalization. Unlike other theorists who are part of his inner circle, McLaren even refers to "ecological disasters." However, he does not go on to consider the characteristics of communities that are less consumer and technology dependent, and whether or not these characteristics would be strengthened by his reform proposals.

The main concern here is whether his assumptions—which represent continual change as a linear form of progress, critical inquiry as the *only* valid source of knowledge, and the right of expert theorists to dismiss the practices and values of different cultural groups as expressions of false consciousness that hide the real history of class and gender oppression—are what give McLaren's analysis its appeal to readers who share the same culturally specific assumptions. The evidence is overwhelming that this is the case. As these are also the assumptions that underlie the Industrial Revolution's relentless pursuit of new markets by undermining traditional forms of communal knowledge and interdependence, it becomes necessary to assess McLaren's references to ending all forms of oppression (which he equates with all traditions) in a new light. It should also be noted that the assumptions McLaren shares with the earlier phase of the Industrial Revolution are the same assumptions that underlie the motivation for developing new software programs intended to displace the culturally diverse traditions of the commons with the monoculture of cyberspace.

McLaren's criticism of essentialism in current thinking about multicultural education is basically sound. But his own position, which, he claims, takes into account the importance of multiple traditions of knowledge as well as his concern with a radical transformation of society, is self-contradictory in several important ways. First, while he argues for a form of education that incorporates cultural differences in ways of knowing, he assumes that marginalized cultural groups will interpret the achievement of social justice in a way that corresponds to his Enlightenment vision; that is, they will rely on critical reflection as the guardian against the oppressiveness of tradition.

Another distinguishing characteristic of his analysis is that while he refers to culture, he never identifies the specific patterns of thinking, metacommunication, intergenerational communication, mythopoetic narratives, moral reciprocity, and technological practices that are shared in varying degrees by members of a cultural group. He will undoubtedly interpret this criticism as based on essentialist thinking—that is, he will think I am assuming that all members of a cultural group share a specific set of traditions. I recognize, however, that members of cultural groups range in their beliefs from the assimilated stance, in which a sense of cultural identity is largely a matter of looking back on the traditions of previous generations, to traditionally oriented members who consciously resist the pressures of modernization. Nevertheless, there remain shared traditions that members reenact, identify with, and individualize.

If there were no shared traditions, there would be no need to recommend, as McLaren does, that "we . . . legitimize multiple traditions of knowledge." To restate the main criticism of McLaren's vision of social justice: by not identifying concrete manifestations of "traditions of knowledge," he does not have to explain the contradiction between legitimating "multiple traditions of knowledge" and his vision of emancipation that "develops out of the imperatives of freedom, liberation, democracy, and critical citizenship" (1995:48). Democracy, as the Iroquois League taught us several centuries ago, can be practiced in cultures that do not share the Western assumptions about change, individualism, and critical reflection as the only legitimate source of knowledge. Democracy can also be practiced in cultures in which there is an ongoing debate over how far assimilation should be carried. It can even be argued that people who want to resist adopting the "antitradition traditions" that characterize the elite are just as legitimate practitioners of democracy as modern theorists who embrace an individualistic and modern lifestyle.

That members of different cultural groups have the same right to express their preference for traditional ways as the members who have more modern preferences raises a second problem inherent in McLaren's messianic way of thinking. Does McLaren's emancipatory approach to aligning curricular and pedagogical decisions with the achievement of a Western view of social justice strengthen the assimilationist position or the ability of cultural groups to resist the form of individual subjectivity required by the digital phase of the Industrial Revolution? When McLaren addresses the systemic sources of injustice, he is highly critical of the deeply rooted connections between "white terror" and the capitalist system. He is also critical of the distortions caused by modern values—particularly those that contribute to the inability to resist the pathologies connected with unlimited consumption. Yet the values and ways of thinking that he acknowledges as important are contradicted by his appeal for "a universal emancipatory world view." In the same passage where this phrase appears, he also argues for the "practices of solidarity and community" (1995:59). As I noted earlier, the contradiction is not recognized because his language is based on schemata of understanding so biased against all expressions of tradition that he is unable to recognize that the "practices of solidarity and community" involve the reenactment of traditions. Indeed, the word *community,* if it is used to refer to a group whose members have sustained each other over four generations (or cohorts), is nearly synonymous with *tradition.*

The following observation by the late Eduardo Grillo on the connections between "nonsubjecthood" and cultural affirmation makes an even stronger argument that traditions cannot be categorized as always being in opposition to social justice. Writing about the efforts of Proyecto Andino de Tecnologías Campesinas to regenerate the Andean worldview, including its traditional agricultural practices, Grillo explains the revolutionary nature of "cultural affirmation": "to decolonize ourselves is to affirm our Andean culture and to reject the imperialistic pretensions of homogenizing peoples. Consequently, to decolonize ourselves is to break with the global enterprise of development" (1998:232).

The affirmation of Andean culture (tradition) means, among

other things, recovering the ability to participate in the reciprocal process of nurturing and letting oneself be nurtured. Part of this tradition is learning to listen—which is very different from the existential stance of critical inquiry. As one Bolivian peasant put it, the Andean mindset requires listening to "the voice of nature itself which announces to us the manner in which we must plant our crops." Again, it must be emphasized that this affirmation of traditional patterns as a source of resistance to the colonizing character of modernization should not be interpreted as a recommendation to embrace all traditions indiscriminately. The Andean program is simply an example of a democratic decolonizing practice aimed toward the regeneration of tradition rather than toward the continual politicizing and relativizing of tradition through constant critical reflection and demystification—which leaves the final authority in the subjective judgment of the supposedly autonomous individual. There are many destructive traditions in both modern and more traditionally oriented cultures. McLaren, however, does not provide a basis for making this crucial distinction. His language turns emancipation into a formula that fails to take account of the nature of relationships and knowledge found in morally and ecologically coherent communities. While he claims to speak in behalf of a multicultural world, his formula is to be universally applied. To reiterate a point made earlier, his formula for emancipation is based on the same assumptions that the Luddites rejected when they rebelled against the industrial system that was being imposed on them by a group of elite thinkers who also viewed themselves as apostles of modern progress.

With the recent death of Paulo Freire, Henry Giroux now shares with Peter McLaren the position of most prominent interpreter of critical pedagogy. Like McLaren, Giroux views all aspects of human existence as embedded in historically conditioned matrices of controlling relationships. Thus, all patterns of human existence, regardless of cultural group, need to be made explicit and, to use his favorite metaphor, "interrogated" in order to emancipate individuals. In effect, the political processes that subjugate individuals need to be transformed into the politics of liberation. This transformative process is not to be the responsibility of parents or the community, but of teachers who possess an understanding of the social vision consistent with the practice of a critical pedagogy. "The pedagogical issue here," Giroux explains, "is the need to articulate difference as part of the construction of a new type of subject, one which would be both multiple and democratic" (1997:152).

While Giroux warns against the dangers of adopting the Enlightenment view that represents rationality as free of historical conditioning and of universalizing prescriptions for reform, he continually ignores his own warnings in explaining how teachers are to politicize the students' taken-for-granted traditions. That Giroux views the social goals and method of critical pedagogy as universally applicable is evident in the following statement:

> Teachers need to take up criticism from within, to develop pedagogical practices that heighten the possibilities not only for critical consciousness but also for transformative action. In this perspective, teachers would be involved in the invention of critical discourses and democratic social relations. Critical pedagogy would represent itself as the active construction rather than the transmission of particular ways of life. More specifically, as transformative intellectuals, teachers could engage in the invention of languages so as to provide spaces for themselves and their students to rethink their experiences in terms that both name relations of oppression and offer ways in which to overcome them. (1997:224)

Especially noteworthy is that this statement contains no guidelines for helping teachers identify the traditions that should *not* be politicized and reconstructed. To reiterate a key point in Giroux's statement, the goal of critical pedagogy is the "active construction" rather than the "transmission" of a particular way of life. For a theorist who claims to speak on behalf of the social justice interests of numerous cultural groups, including people who have chosen to carry forward the traditions of their communities, this is an incredibly arrogant statement. Indeed, it is difficult to see in it any sensitivity to his own warning about universal prescriptions of social reform.

Like McLaren's, Giroux's use of language organizes the world into the dualistic categories of victims of oppressive traditions and individuals who achieve greater autonomy by constructing their own knowledge and value systems (under the guidance of critical pedagogy teachers). Further, Giroux equates democracy with the process of demystifying all aspects of cultural life—a formula that is to be applied to all cultures. By equating democracy with the emancipation of students he excludes parents and other citizens from the process. Their traditions and personal interests, by his definition, have not been continually reconstructed through the process of critical inquiry that teachers ("transformative intellectuals") control.

It is difficult to understand why so many readers fail to recognize that Giroux's continual references to the need to create democratic public spheres are no more than linguistic rituals intended to give legitimacy to his narrow view of democracy. He may genuinely believe that he is contributing to more democratic public spheres, but only the people who agree with his assumption that equates continual change (supposedly the outcome of critical reflection) with progress and democracy will be recognized as the new "type of subject" that the educational process is to create. This dualism, which Carl Schmitt refers to as the friend/enemy approach to politics, carries over to the personal practices of McLaren, Giroux, and other critical pedagogy theorists. While they praise the importance of dialogue, they ignore anyone who disagrees with their point of view—and have even gone so far as to label them fascists.

The deep cultural schemata Giroux inherited from the philosophers and social theorists who laid the conceptual foundations for modern consciousness surface in his view of the nature of customs—a term he uses as roughly equivalent to traditions. His abstract way of representing all customs (traditions) as problematic is especially noteworthy. That is, he is not challenging just the customs that sustain social inequities; rather, all customs are to be subjected to the critical judgment of students and reconstituted in ways that conform to the students' understanding of social justice. Referring to Bruce James Smith's distinction between remembrance and custom, Giroux goes on to say:

> I want to extend Smith's argument by developing remembrance as a form of counter-memory and custom as a form of reactionary nostalgia rooted in the loss of memory. Custom, as Smith argues, constructs subjects within a discourse of continuity in which knowledge and practice are viewed as a matter of inheritance and transmission. Custom is the complex of ideologies and social practices that views counter-memory as subversive and critical teaching as unpatriotic. It is the ideological basis for forms of knowledge and pedagogy which refuse to interrogate public forms and which deny difference as a fundamental referent for a democratic society. (1997:153–154)

The importance of recognizing "difference" is contradicted by Giroux's blanket indictment of all customs. The irony is that Giroux reenacts a number of customs (traditions) in the very process of encoding his ideas into a print-based form of communication. He also relies on a complex network of customs to ensure both the continuation of his financial security and the right to academic freedom that come with being a member of one of society's most tradition-bound institutions. His own life patterns involve the reenactment of customs that I am certain he would not want to have continually politicized and renegotiated. The fact that his abstract theory does not take into account the multiple customs that are part of his own taken-for-granted sense of everyday reality is not the critical point here. Yet it deserves mention in order to highlight the limitations of using language that is so abstract and distorted that it no longer represents the complexity of human interdependencies.

More to the point is that categorizing all customs (traditions) as reactionary, mindless habits and oppressive practices cannot be the basis for a pedagogy that contributes to a socially just society. According to Giroux's way of thinking, all members of society, regardless of cultural background and degree of participation in their primary and secondary cultures, must be willing to yield to the moral judgments of students and their teachers. In the 1930s, George Counts urged teachers to become a selfless vanguard dedicated to the task of creating a new social order. More recently, the world has witnessed several examples of student-led revolutionary movements that set out to overturn all traditions. Few people today would agree that the Red Guard and the youthful followers of Pol Pot created democratic public spheres that provided for greater social equality and the discovery of new personal identities. The followers of McLaren and Giroux seem to overlook the irony that the doctrine of continual change (even if it were possible) and the blanket indictment of all customs are based on a deeper assumption about the nature of progress that Giroux shares with Western technologists who have also committed themselves to reconstructing traditions—but in the image of the machine that requires the constant attention of a different class of experts.

Giroux shares with McLaren a deep concern with the role language plays in determining how the ecology of power plays out to the advantage of some while disadvantaging others. Drawing on the linguistic insights of Paulo Freire (which are far shallower than his followers recognize) and the Russian linguist Mikhail Bakhtin, Giroux opens up an area of inquiry that should be the central focus of study in all teacher education programs. Unfortunately, the Enlightenment assumptions encoded in his political metaphors prevent him from recognizing how the formulaic and utopian nature of his analysis is framed by the language he uses. That is, language, especially the political metaphors that reproduce earlier processes of analogic thinking framed by the prevailing root metaphors, directs his supposedly rational analysis far more than he realizes. Giroux is not the only theorist caught in this double bind. McLaren, Michael Apple, Ira Shor, and even Freire base their analyses and prescriptions on the use of political metaphors so widely used that the historical misconceptions they encode are no longer recognized.

Perhaps the most problematic use of a political metaphor is the way McLaren, Giroux, and other theorists use the word *conservative*. The analogues associated with this word include educators who want to "transmit" a definite body of knowledge that "celebrates the logic of the marketplace," corporations that want to maintain a form of education that facilitates the further exploitation of the working class, and anyone who opposes racial and gender equality and democratic decision making.

Their use of *conservative* is problematic for two reasons. First, the Enlightenment assumptions and values that Giroux and the others associate with conservatism are the very ones that the Luddites viewed as destroying the self-sufficient and interdependent nature of their communities. Only revisionist historians like those who claim that the Holocaust did not occur would insist that the Luddites were precursors of modern liberal thinkers. William Morris, a leading British socialist in the latter part of the nineteenth century, argued that the recovery and conservation of communal craft and agricultural knowledge represented the only viable alternative to the dehumanizing effects of liberal/industrial thinking. The Arts and Crafts movement he helped to establish reflects a concern with a basic social justice issue that is becoming even more pressing today: the need to regenerate community traditions and relationships that nurture the talents and skills of members.

Second, other leading advocates of social justice who would never be regarded as liberal and emancipatory thinkers are not hard to find. Gandhi, for example, based his vision of postcolonial India on the recovery of self-sufficient villages and towns and on the traditional customs of moral reciprocity within these communities. His critique of modernity can easily be translated today into a critique of the liberal assumptions encoded in Giroux's political metaphors—including Giroux's decontextualized representation of democracy as centered in the process of critical inquiry and emancipation from all customs (traditions).

The key assumptions underlying modern liberalism—the authority of the individual's subjective judgment, the relentless pursuit of innovative ideas, individual-centered values and forms of expression, disregard for traditions, a proclivity to think in abstractions that lend themselves to being universalized—all lead to an increasingly experimental form of culture. This cultural form, which today finds expression in the use of modern ideologies to design societies and new organisms that further the process of economic globalization, rests on a basic misunderstanding of biological and cultural processes that are inescapable aspects of human existence. The political metaphor that best accounts for these inescapable processes is *conservatism*.

A strong case can be made that conservatism as a political metaphor actually represents the forms of community and community-nature relationships that many marginalized cultural groups consider central to any discussion of social justice. As I have written elsewhere about the need to rectify our political vocabulary as a first step to rectifying our relationships (Bowers 1987, 1995, 1997), I will merely summarize here the inescapable biological and cultural expressions of conservatism as well as its more political forms. First, the inescapable forms of conservatism.

The Conservative Nature of Biological Processes

The process of autopoiesis is seen in the way cells reproduce themselves by interacting with other cells that carry the genetic information that in turn influences how they interact with other cells. For example, the DNA in the cell nucleus produces RNA molecules, which contain instructions for the production of proteins and enzymes that determine tissue and organ development. The genetic instructions within an autopoietic system that reproduce future generations of cells with similar genetic instructions—unless altered by the biochemical changes occurring in the larger network of autopoietic systems—represent a conservative process that is part of the natural world. But it is not a static process. That is, it does not always involve the identical replication of earlier generations. What Richard Dawkins refers to as the "selfish gene" should not be translated to mean that the DNA molecule, like the emancipatory theorists' view of conservatism, is driven by selfish motives. Rather, he means in his use of this easily misleading metaphor that the chemical instructions ensure the replication of the genetic code in future generations. The organic form of conservatism always carries the qualification that other chemical instructions within the autopoietic system may introduce changes—which will then be reproduced in future generations until other changes occur within the system. If we change the scale from cells to organisms, we see the continuity of heritable traits in plants, animals, and human beings. While the process of conservation can also be seen in natural selection, I do not want to suggest that it should serve as an analogue for understanding cultural and political forms of conservatism. Rather, the point is that efforts to categorize conservatism as pathological fail to recognize that it is expressed in our physical makeup and in the natural processes we depend on.

Temperamental Conservatism

At the psychological level of self-identity, personal habits, and preferences (in food, clothing, social relationships, use of language, and other taken-for-granted cultural patterns) we do not see continual change, experimentation with new lifestyle patterns, and continual self "interrogation." Rather, we see that the patterns we are comfortable with tend to be repeated—which is an expression of the conservative nature of our personal lifestyle. There are always changes, but they tend to be minor and not to disrupt the core taken-for-granted basis of our self-concept. A death, divorce, loss of employment, or other major disruption may bring the mosaic of taken-for-granted patterns into question or undermine it entirely. The personal lives of the emancipatory theorists, as well as the lives of Marx, Mao, and other "revolutionary" thinkers, exhibit the inescapable hold of this form of conservatism—even as they proclaim the need to overthrow all expressions of conservatism. Temperamental conservatism is an inherent aspect of personal lifestyle. Although it is heavily influenced by culture, it has no specific political orientation.

Cultural Conservatism

Basically, the language systems that sustain daily cultural life reproduce the patterns essential to the self-identity of the culture's members and influence how they interact with each other. The conservative nature of languaging is evident in the way that the metaphorical language McLaren, Giroux, and other emancipatory theorists use reproduces (conserves) the assumptions of the philosophers and political theorists who helped establish the analogues for individual, new ideas, change, and so forth. We can also see the conservative nature of language in the way the mechanistic root metaphor that underlies Newtonian science continues to frame the thinking of contemporary scientists engaged in brain research. In effect, when we learn the languages of our culture (verbal, patterns of metacommunication, architecture, organization of space, etc.) we simultaneously learn how to interact in ways predictable by other members of the language community. Again, the basic symbolic processes that sustain, renew, and modify cultural patterns, even while members of the culture may make more individualized interpretations of the patterns (and even reject certain ones), are conservative in nature. Edward Shils has observed that even individuals and groups who are dedicated to creating new ways of understanding are, in fact, carrying forward (conserving) a culturally specific tradition of being against traditions—at least those they are aware of.

Economic Conservatism

The popular use of conservatism as a political metaphor that encompasses everyone who thinks in terms of competitive individualism, freedom to expand and exploit markets, and the progressive nature of technology and science shows a lack of understanding of the core beliefs of classical liberalism. To label as conservative the business ethos that is so indifferent to the viability of communities and to marginalized individuals and cultural groups, as McLaren, Giroux, and Apple do, is to create a double bind that has important implications for addressing issues in the more inclusive category of eco-justice.

In effect, their misuse of *conservative* undermines the ability of groups working to regenerate more self-reliant communities and sustainable ecosystems to use the political language that best describes their efforts. For example, in the struggle to limit the adverse impacts of industry on the environment we have scientists who are working as "restoration biologists" and "conservationists." Other environmentalists are engaged in wilderness "preservation." These are essentially conservative activities. Categorizing these people as "liberal" environmentalists puts them into bed with people and institutions that are guided by the liberal ideas and values largely responsible for the crises of community, environment, and cultural homogenization these people are trying to eliminate.

Ironically, and this is the other aspect of the double bind, emancipatory educational theorists share with groups they mislabel as conservative the beliefs and values that lead to a highly experimental approach to cultural development—and to the creation of a world monoculture. A form of democracy based on the assumption that *all* cultural patterns must be continually "interrogated" represents an experiment that opens the door to totalitarian systems. The increasingly dominant nature of modern technology involves a similar orientation; but instead of continual critical reflection and interrogation, technology's antitradition orientation is expressed in the incessant search for technologies that can be substituted for organic processes. It is simply, as Lewis Mumford warned decades ago, another form of totalitarianism—one that hides behind the guise of searching for the most cost-effective systems of human control and predication.

Philosophical Conservatism

This tradition of reflective conservatism goes back to Edmund Burke's writings on how to ensure that ideas about change take into account the constructive and mutually supportive aspects of community, including how communities have incorporated an understanding of the bioregion into their traditions. The more contemporary philosophical conservatives exhibit a dialectical way of thinking that addresses the many expressions of extremism. If too much emphasis is placed on the authority of abstract ideas, they will argue for the recovery of experientially based knowledge. If traditions are interpreted as static and as sources of absolute authority, they will argue for more freedom of individual expression and for the importance of change as a form of renewal. And if too much stress is placed on change and individuals constructing their own knowledge from direct experience, they will explain that we are embedded in cultural traditions and that some of these traditions are sources of empowerment and social justice.

Their more complex view of human nature, which recognizes the historical record of both altruism and rationalism, leads them to adopt a more cautious stance toward theories that are based on assumptions about individuals always acting in ways that are beneficial to the community. Thus they urge that political systems be based on the separation of powers, and checks and balances. Unlike McLaren, Giroux, Freire, and Dewey, who assume that if people are educated to the right way of thinking they will always act in socially constructive ways, the philosophical conservative points to the historical record of individuals who have turned the Enlightenment way of thinking toward selfish and manipulative ends.

Cultural/Bio-Conservatism

This is the form of conservatism exhibited by indigenous cultures that have adapted their technologies and communal patterns to live in ways that do not degrade the self-renewing capacities of the environment. Indeed, their awareness that their survival depends on

the viability of natural systems is one of the distinguishing characteristics of this form of conservatism. It is the form of conservatism
expressed in the writings of Vandana Shiva, Wendell Berry, Gary
Snyder, and others who are attempting to clarify the interdependencies that exist between individuals, communities, and natural
systems. As a guiding ideology that takes many forms of cultural
expression, cultural/bio-conservatism also provides the conceptual
and moral basis for a more radical critique of the economic model
of development than can be made by the experimental- and
progress-oriented educational theorists. As *democracy* is as open to
interpretation as *resistance,* a term Giroux used earlier as a rallying
cry, there is little in the thinking of McLaren and Giroux that can be
used to challenge the current rush to turn everyone into a middle-
class consumer. That is, there is little in the emancipatory educators' use of context-free metaphors that members of different
cultural groups can identify with—especially if they, like the
Luddites, are struggling to retain their patterns of community self-
sufficiency.

The observation by Gerald Berthoud quoted in the Introduction
represents one aspect of the cultural/bio-conservative way of understanding the basic relationship missing in the thinking of the
emancipatory educational theorists. The key part of his statement
is that the networks of solidarity (which are usually based on traditions of intergenerational responsibility) are undermined by the
"notion that human life, if it is to be fully realized, cannot be *con-
strained by limits of any kind*" (italics added). Among the questions
this observation raises are the following:

What limits to individual emancipation are recognized by
McLaren, Giroux, and others who think in the context-free
metaphors that serve as code words for a supposedly revolutionary pedagogy?

Do they recognize the limits established by an increasingly
fragile environment?

Do they recognize the limits that are integral to participating in different cultural approaches to networks of solidarity?

Finally, do they recognize that different cultural groups, even those who have assimilated aspects of modern consciousness and technology, may view unresolved social justice issues in radically different ways?

The inability of McLaren and Giroux to ground their reform proposals in terms that take account of the actual patterns and beliefs of cultural groups that have not allowed themselves to be homogenized within the dominant culture is a major reason why they continue to frame social justice issues in terms of a "universalist emancipatory world view"—to quote McLaren again. Until they integrate into their theories of education the traditions of solidarity and mutual aid that are distinctive to different cultural groups, their efforts to universalize critical inquiry as the only pathway to knowledge and empowerment will become yet another expression of Western cultural domination.

Michael Apple and Jean Anyon

Michael Apple and Jean Anyon take a different approach to social justice issues by focusing directly on how schools, in reflecting the structural characteristics dictated by the economic interests, continue to privilege a certain segment of society while further marginalizing other segments. This more grounded analysis of Apple is summed up in his observation that

> everything I have said . . . requires that we place even our best efforts at educational "reform" back into the macro- and micro-relations of power inside schools, and between schools and the relations of exploitation and domination that provide the social context in which education operates. . . . We need to be concerned not only with whose knowledge gets to be declared "official" and what identities are

formed—central questions in the debates over the politics of culture—but also with what discursive resources circulate that enable
people to understand the world and their place in it. Economic discourse, organized around *conservative* agendas, plays a large part as a
primary cultural resource for people to "know their place" . . . in the
world. (1996:104, 115–116; italics added)

I italicized Apple's use of the word *conservative* to highlight the confusion he introduces into the analysis and to stress how some readers might interpret his recommendation that the school curriculum incorporate the knowledge of cultural groups that he views as
now being excluded. Does Apple really mean that unrestricted capitalism, with its technological and scientific support systems, is a
conservative force? Does the use of a political category he associates
with exploitation and domination mean that the knowledge and
identities of excluded cultural groups must be stripped of their
conservative elements? How can a social justice pedagogy be taken
seriously if its mission is to use the curriculum to create the Western form of self-identity and mindset that a liberal educator like
Apple can feel comfortable with? These are not meant as rhetorical
questions; rather, they foreground an area of silence he shares
with McLaren, Giroux, Freire, and Dewey. Apple's analysis of how
schools reproduce the distinction between high- and low-status
knowledge essential to the economic system should be taken seriously. However, his failure to understand that any discussion of
knowledge, values, and identities must take into account differences
in cultures prevents him from framing his prescriptions for reform
in ways that will strengthen cultural diversity in American society.
It is also important to note that Apple continues to frame social
justice issues in ways that ignore the rapid changes occurring in the
viability of natural systems that scientists have been documenting
over the last thirty years. In short, his criticisms of capitalism,
which he represents as the primary source of class divisions and

domination, do not include an analysis of how education can contribute to less commodified, more intergenerationally responsible communities.

The economic determinism argument is less visible in Anyon's way of framing how educators should address the structural aspects of poverty and limited opportunity experienced by large segments of American society. In *Ghetto Schooling: A Political Economy of Urban Educational Reform* (1997), Anyon examines the history of discrimination and economic marginalization experienced by African Americans in Newark, New Jersey, by carefully documenting how population, economic, and political trends relate to their continued state of impoverishment. She recommends a wide range of reforms in the education of teachers that will help reverse the public schools' complicity in maintaining racial segregation, job discrimination, and general cultural marginalization. She even lists a number of concrete steps that educational reforms should take, such as working with community development organizations and legal services groups. Unlike the approach of McLaren and Giroux, whose decontextualized theory and unrecognized Enlightenment assumptions involve fundamental contradictions, Anyon's case study approach foregrounds the complexity of the issues educational reformers must deal with. It also leads to specific recommendations that avoid the hidden intergenerational conflict that accompanies the emancipatory theorists' emphasis on students deconstructing the traditions of their parents and other community members in the name of direct democracy and a universal vision of liberation.

While Anyon's case study approach is framed by her concern with the economic basis of socially unjust practices, it could also be used to highlight how other cultural groups, in terms of their histories of interaction with the dominant Euro-American culture, view forms of social injustice that go beyond issues of class, race, and gender. For example, the physical landscape of what indigenous people called Turtle Island was integrated into the conceptual and moral landscapes thousands of years before European adventurers and settlers arrived. The loss of the land, the basis of their self-sufficient communities and their symbolic heritage, continues today to be an unresolved source of social injustice that may be far more critical to them than the trilogy of injustices most educational reformers focus on. Cultural groups centered on renewing traditions of intergenerational knowledge and responsibility (what the Mexican writer Carlos Fuentes refers to as "the strength of the past in the present") may experience the emancipatory educators' attempts to frame social justice issues in ways that foster greater individual autonomy as a further betrayal of their right to carry forward their traditions. The modern agenda of expanding a secular, technological, consumer, and expert-knowledge-based world, a central part of the high-status knowledge learned in public schools and universities, creates numerous double binds for cultural groups that still retain values and ways of thinking that separate them from the culture of modernism. The threat to their values and basic beliefs has pushed some groups to acts of extreme resistance. For example, young people are putting themselves at physical risk in order to protect old-growth forests from further devastation by individuals and corporations who think primarily in economic terms. Indeed, this form of political activism, which now has a global reach, does not fit neatly into the educator's categories of class, race, and gender.

The latter example brings us back to the question of why educational theorists, with few exceptions, frame social justice issues in a way that ignores the physical destruction and toxic contamination of the environment. To reiterate, their language continues to reproduce assumptions shared by both Enlightenment thinkers and promoters of the Industrial Revolution. These assumptions include: the autonomous individual who uses rational thought either to deconstruct the hold of tradition on the assumption that change guarantees a more progressive future or as a means of creating technologies; a human-centered perspective that views Nature as either a resource or a background so insignificant that it can be left out of any discussion of the human situation; a use of language that is disconnected from place and is generally misrepresented as a sender-receiver model of communication; and the use of the personal pronoun *I* in a way that locates observations, values, and relationships as centered in the subjectivity of individual judgment.

Another reason for their narrow interpretation of social justice can be found in the traditions of thought they have borrowed so heavily from. Marx, for example, viewed peasant cultures with utter contempt and borrowed a distorted interpretation of evolution from Darwin that shut off the possibility that reform could be based on learning from cultures that had taken nonindustrial approaches to development. More recent European theorists often quoted by emancipatory educators continue to frame their analyses of cultural domination and their prescriptions for reform in ways that carry on the long tradition of Western philosophy that overemphasizes the transforming power of theory. By ignoring the ecological crisis these European theorists avoid addressing issues related to the burgeoning world population, the economic and technological dominance of the North, the ways new technologies centralize control over who has access to work, the need to regenerate communities that have a smaller ecological footprint, and the need to develop an awareness that individual freedom should not be expressed in ways that undermine the diversity and self-renewing capacity of the Earth's natural systems. Important European thinkers such as Arne Naess, Edward Goldsmith, Wolfgang Sachs, and Helena Norberg-Hodge do address these issues, but they are not mentioned in the writings of McLaren, Giroux, Apple, Shor, and others who refuse to acknowledge the disproportionate suffering experienced by marginalized cultural groups in North America and the Third World.

Paulo Freire and John Dewey

A few comments are in order on how the intellectual legacies of Paulo Freire and John Dewey contribute to the double binds inherent in how emancipatory educational theorists think about social justice issues. As the secularizing influence of science will continue to be one of the dominant characteristics of the high-status knowledge promoted in North American universities, philosophers and educational theorists will continue to find Dewey's pragmatism and process orientation an important source of guidance for their own thinking. For this reason, Dewey, rather than Freire, is the more likely to have a lasting influence on how educational reform is understood. With the exception of the critical pedagogy theorists who continue to identify themselves more directly with Freire, his influence has waned significantly in the past few years.

Among Dewey's most often cited contributions are his emphases on learning participatory decision making, overcoming the separation of schooling from the life of the community, using the school as the source of a common learning experience that helps overcome ethnic and social class distinctions, and viewing the school as an agency of progressive reform. When stated in these general terms, Dewey's educational goals appear highly relevant to the core social problems of today. Unfortunately, most educational theorists, including philosophers such as Richard Rorty, do not recognize that his ideas are based on culturally specific assumptions that are now being challenged. The most important challenges come from minority cultures' open resistance to being homogenized into the dominant culture for which Dewey was a spokesperson and the growing awareness that modern progress is undermining the viability of natural systems.

One of Dewey's central concerns was to bring students and the different elements of community together in problem-solving situations in which they would learn to use the "method of intelligence" as the basis of collective decision making. As Dewey explains in *The Quest for Certainty* (1929), the only valid approach to thinking, including the determination of values that are to guide social action, is the scientific method. Dewey did not qualify his position on this crucial point. Unfortunately, his followers have not seen the need to question the classroom extrapolations that seem, on the surface, consistent with the Deweyian position that all beliefs, values, and traditions of the community should be treated as relative—and thus subject to continual reconstruction. Indeed, Dewey and his followers hold that the highest educational attainment is to develop an increased capacity to reconstruct the conceptual and moral underpinning of community life. As I pointed out earlier in this chapter, Dewey's followers proclaim their commitment to cultural diversity in the classroom, and thus in the larger society, but ignore the fact that many of the ethnic groups they seek to emancipate from domination do not view their own beliefs and values as in need of reconstruction.

To summarize, Dewey's ideas are inconsistent with a social justice pedagogy that addresses, in addition to race, class, and gender issues, the right of other cultural groups in American society to retain traditions essential to their identity, forms of communal solidarity and mutual aid, and spiritual centeredness. For example, Dewey viewed differences in cultural ways of knowing, as he experienced them among the immigrants living in Chicago and New York City, against the yardstick of his own early life in Vermont and his later experiences in middle-class circles in which critical reflection and participatory decision making were, on the surface, the modus operandi. Immigrants who held onto their traditional ways of thinking were seen as inadequately integrated into American society, and thus unable to participate fully in the democratic process. Dewey failed to recognize that the type of individual needed for the continual reconstruction of collective experience must possess many of the same qualities that were essential to the success of the Industrial Revolution. That is, Dewey's ideal individual would not view traditions as providing answers to questions of relationships and responsibilities. Rather, the existential orientation would be toward change and the creation of new ideas and values. Nor did Dewey recognize the extent to which his own experiences involved the reenactment of cultural traditions taken for granted in his day. A classroom based on his ideas would question traditions, reconstructing them to fit the problem-solving needs of the group and ignoring what is not viewed as problematic—all of which would contribute to weakening the ethnic students' commitment to their cultural traditions.

Furthermore, Dewey's insistence that there is only one method of intelligence, as well as his habit of denigrating tradition-centered cultures (he refers to them as "savages" in *Democracy and Education* [1916:396]), reinforces the modern, scientific mindset that views the knowledge embedded in indigenous cultures as having too little merit to warrant learning it. Dewey's bias also disregards the forms of learning that take place in mainstream communities where skills, ceremonies, and other noncommodified forms of relationships are intergenerationally shared. Few students in a Deweyian–critical pedagogy–constructivist classroom would be able to recognize the difference between an older person and an elder, or understand the importance of elder knowledge to the moral ecology of the community.

If we think in terms of the more inclusive category of an eco-justice pedagogy, we find Dewey's ideas falling short, and even contributing to the crisis. Even the best interpretation of Dewey's ideas of growth, participatory decision making, and the scientific method of problem solving, which involves both a human-centered view of nature and each generation constructing its own responses to emerging problems, leads to an eco-management approach to environmental problems that is profoundly different from the systems of moral reciprocity with Nature that many indigenous cultures have developed. Modern cultural patterns of representing self-restraint (particularly in behalf of the environment and our own future generations) as old-fashioned and subversive of the form of individualism needed to "grow the economy" lead to degraded natural systems that then require an eco-management system. In effect, Dewey's ideas are relevant to coping with the problem after it has reached a state of extreme crisis, but not to preventing the crisis in the first place.

As an early spokesperson for the highest values of Western modernity, including some values and social practices that have genuine merit, Dewey cannot be turned into a deep ecology thinker. Thus, his ideas cannot be the basis of educational reform that addresses the deep cultural roots of the ecological crisis. The primary reason for this is that his theory of intelligence lacks an understanding of how language reproduces earlier, pre-ecological ways of thinking. Nor can his equation of growth with the ability to reconstruct experience be easily reconciled with the need to regenerate the noncommodified traditions of community. Lastly, the changes in the environment are signaling that there are moral limits, while Dewey's philosophy tells us that moral relationships are a matter of perspective and continual change, and must be judged in terms of their instrumental value. The latter is not always a matter of consensus, especially when the moral judgments of cultural groups do not correspond to Dewey's assumptions about the efficacy of the scientific method for determining values in a secular universe.

Many of these criticisms of Dewey also apply to the ideas of Paulo Freire. Like Dewey, Freire's contributions are undermined by the Enlightenment assumptions he takes for granted. As Freire has been accorded a status among emancipatory educational theorists that has been elevated above criticism, I want to state at the outset that there are specific social conditions in which the use of his pedagogy would be appropriate. These would include situations in which a cultural group has been under colonial rule, when the internal cultural patterns organize the distribution of wealth and political power in ways that subject part of the population to poverty, and when traditions of gender and age bias are restrictive and denigrating. I also want to affirm the importance of Freire's emphasis on dialogue and his understanding of the political nature of language. It should be pointed out, however, that it was Martin Buber who presented the more complex and adequate explanation of dialogue—including its fragile nature. Similarly, Freire's argument for making critical inquiry a central part of the educational process can be traced back to earlier proponents of a liberal education. Thus, I do not diminish the importance of these two characteristics of a sound approach to education when I criticize Freire as a proponent of a modernizing, Western form of consciousness.

Like nearly all Western philosophers, Freire bases his arguments on a view of the rational process and human nature that does not take into account the profound differences that exist in cultural ways of knowing. For example, the assumption that there is a universal human nature—a central part of his argument in *Pedagogy of the Oppressed* (1971) and *Education for Critical Consciousness* (1973)—ignores the ways the mythopoetic narratives of different cultures frame how identities, relationships, and the natural world are understood within these cultures. When we analyze his view of what it means to be fully human we find that it corresponds to the Enlightenment idea of the rational, self-determining individual who lives in a world of progressive change. This view of human nature is evident in his description of the qualities of "critically transitive consciousness"—the phrase he uses for the fully engaged human being. "Critical transitivity," he writes in *Education for Critical Consciousness*, is "characteristic of authentically democratic regimes and corresponds to highly permeable, interrogative, restless and dialogical forms of life—in contrast to silence and inaction" (1973:18–19). This Enlightenment way of equating change with progress and of thinking of critical reflection as the primary basis for initiating change can also be seen in the following quotation from Freire's most widely acclaimed book, *Pedagogy of the Oppressed:*

> Human existence cannot be silent, nor can it be nourished by false words, but only by true words, with which men transform the world. To exist, humanly, is to name the world, to change it. Once named, the world in its turn reappears to the namers as problem and requires of them a new naming. Men are not built in silence, but in word, in work, in action-reflection.
>
> But while to say the true word—which is work, which is praxis—is to transform the world, saying that word is not the privilege of some few men, but the right of every man. Consequently, no one can say a true word alone—nor can he say it for another, in a prescriptive act which robs others of their words. (1971:76)

The reference to a universal human nature rather than to the actual patterns of individual-community relationships among the cultural groups of Central America, Africa, India, or Southeast Asia represents the same modern way of thinking that is found in transnational corporations' view of global markets. This abstract way of thinking misrepresents a fundamental reality: namely, that the everyday life of people is nested in a particular set of cultural traditions, and that these traditions are continually tested by changes taking place in the environment. Some of the traditions are well attuned to the characteristics of the environment and to the needs of the community, while others may have a long-term destructive impact. In effect, the Platonic tendency in Freire's thinking leads him to ignore the specific traditions that need to be renamed. Nor does he address which cultures should have their entire conceptual and moral foundations renamed by successive generations of critical reflection. It is also important to note that Freire's ideal of the critically reflective individual would not be encumbered with the community-centered values and responsibilities that characterized the kind of community that the Luddites were struggling to preserve. Rather, by identifying critical reflection as the only source of legitimate knowledge, and by framing the characteristics of the emancipated individual within a culturally specific view of temporality that emphasizes that change is always a progressive movement away from the constraints of tradition, Freire's pedagogy leads to a rootless individual who is easily manipulated by the media and other commercial interests. The university-educated elites within the corporate world also understand the political nature of language and know how to use language to shape the expectations and identities of individuals who have been socialized to think of themselves as existing in a human-centered world of constant change. The modern assumptions underlying Freire's pedagogy, as well as that of his followers, simply make their task easier.

The following list gives a summary of the limitations of Freire's thinking.

His emphasis on viewing humans as possessing a universal essence represents an Enlightenment way of thinking that ignores the need to take into account cultural differences as well as the complex moral issues that accompany imposing a Western view of morality on non-Western cultures.

His view of the nature of change ignores the different ways in which cultural groups interpret the nature of the past (traditions) and its relationship to the present and future.

By recognizing critical reflection as the only genuine source of knowledge, which is one of the chief characteristics of a print-based form of consciousness, Freire delegitimates other forms of knowledge and intergenerational communication that are often the basis of mutually supportive communities.

The anthropocentrism (human-centeredness) that underlies his pedagogy, while largely unnoticed by Western thinkers, would further undermine cultures that have developed complex systems of interspecies communication and moral reciprocity with the natural world.

Equally abstract statements about the importance of dialogue, consciousness raising, and "transforming the world" have a positive ring to Western theorists—and to Third World theorists who have been educated in Western universities. Unfortunately, abstract thinking about an ideal world too often becomes an excuse for not undertaking the more difficult challenge of framing strategies of educational empowerment in ways that take account of the distinctive characteristics of the local context. Proposals for reform need to consider which traditions of a cultural group need to be renewed and strengthened, and which are morally problematic and thus in need of being reformed or entirely abandoned. It is interesting to note that Esteva and Prakash, writing from a Third World perspective, make no reference to Freire's ideas. The reason may be found in their observation that "people's experiences at the grassroots cannot be reduced to any single new political theory or a global political counter-proposal" (1998:167). This observation, as well as Majid Rahnema's concern that the use of Freire's pedagogy has too often led to the charge that grassroots resistance to the vanguard's idea of revolutionary change is the expression of "counter-revolutionary influences" (1992:125), raises the even more complex issue of how to reconcile local values and traditions of interdependency with externally imposed approaches to reform.

Not even the god-word *emancipation* is an adequate justification for intervening in the beliefs and values of cultural groups faced with an environment that is less and less able to support the growing demands being placed on it. Instead of thinking of emancipation as being from intergenerational knowledge and moral constraints relating to how to live within the limits of the environment, perhaps emancipation should be from the influence of Western technologies and the modernizing ideology—which could be justified in the name of ecological sustainability. Current followers of Freire and Dewey fail to grasp the importance of including cultural differences in any discussion of what constitutes a social justice–oriented pedagogy. As they are likely to claim that their current emphasis on "revolutionary multiculturalism" invalidates this criticism, I want to restate that their inability to acknowledge other forms of knowledge than that derived through critical inquiry in their theory of a critical pedagogy remains a fundamental limitation. They also fail to recognize that eco-justice is the more encompassing challenge, and that it will require an approach that is sensitive to the need to strengthen the local cultural traditions of noncommodified community life.

2 The Limitations of Science as the Basis for an Eco-Justice Pedagogy

There is a long tradition in North America of using the sciences to justify educational reforms. Before assessing how educators' past and present interpretations of science have diverted attention away from unresolved cultural and ecological issues, it will be useful to summarize the essential characteristics of an eco-justice pedagogy. The summary will provide a basis for keeping the characteristics of an eco-justice pedagogy in the forefront of an analysis that could easily mislead us as to what our reform priorities should be. First, the form it takes, in terms of pedagogy and curriculum, cannot be formulated as the "one best way" for all cultures. Instead, it must take into account local traditions—including local knowledge of place. Second, it must clarify for students the dynamics of how technologies promoted by elite groups and hyperconsumerist strategies contribute to environmental racism and to undermining the heritage of minority cultures. Third, it must include intergenerational knowledge of the practices and values that contribute to mutual aid and networks of solidarity within the community and with neighboring communities. Fourth, it must view the regeneration of less-commodified activities and relationships as a process of balancing a critique of destructive ways of thinking (including technological practices) with an effort to help students understand and (when possible) participate in community activities that develop personal talents and a sense of responsibility toward the well-being of others. The latter is less likely to be strengthened through abstract, print-based forms of communication and learning than through participating in relationships centered on an activity of mutual interest.

In the last two chapters I explain in greater detail the curricular and pedagogical implications of an eco-justice pedagogy in the contexts of urban and rural North America. The question at issue here is whether the multiple dimensions of science—as a way of knowing, as a series of genuine achievements, and as an increasingly influential metanarrative that is delegitimating traditional sources of moral authority of the world's cultures—can lead to the development of an eco-justice pedagogy. Or is science propelling us further in the headlong rush toward the ecological catastrophe that will result from globalizing the Western consumer lifestyle? As science is making important contributions to our understanding of the scale of the ecological crisis and improving some aspects in the quality of daily life while it creates weapons of mass destruction and technologies that contaminate the environment, there can never be a simple answer to that question. And whether affirmative or negative, it will always be based on privileging certain priorities over others, and will thus be an expression of the ideology of the person who formulates the answer. Yet, the increasingly dominant role that scientists play in shaping the direction of the world's cultures cannot be left out of any serious discussion of educational reform.

Educational theorists who extrapolate from various areas of science specific approaches to teaching and curriculum reform are, in effect, proposing that scientists' understanding of reality should be the basis of reforming education and, by extension, society itself. Thus, both the educational theorists' understanding of scientific theories and research and the larger question of whether science should be viewed as providing the moral framework that all cultures should adopt are the central concerns of this chapter.

The attempts of previous generations of educational theorists in America to use science as the basis of reform do not constitute a success story. Indeed, the record is long on dismal failures and short on successes. The desire to put education on a scientific basis was one of the earliest goals that led to the field of educational psychology—which still does not recognize the cultural nature of intelligence and the role language plays in reproducing, with remarkably slight variations, patterns of intelligence across the generations. Lewis M. Terman, one of the earliest American contributors to the scientific study of intelligence, started with the assumption that it is possible to measure scientifically the innate intelligence of the individual. He succeeded, through refining the French psychologist Alfred Benet's scale for measuring intelligence, in establishing a tradition within educational psychology of reifying measurement as an objective predictor of a student's intelligence. The racism inherent in his approach has been continued in the more recent writings of Arthur Jensen, Robert J. Herrnstein, and Charles Murray. For example, in *The Bell Curve: Intelligence and Class Structure in American Life* (1994:105), Herrnstein and Murray claim that approximately 60 percent of intelligence can be attributed to genetic inheritance. They further assert that intelligence and achievement tests show that East Asians have "higher nonverbal intelligence than whites," and the "average white person tests higher than about 84 percent of the population of blacks" (269).

The tradition extending from Terman to Herrnstein and Murray represents a tradition of hubris shaped by the cultural bias that is inherent in any attempt to place what is primarily a complex cultural phenomenon on a scientific footing. The inability of science to account for (indeed, its indifference toward) cultural differences in ways of knowing is one of the chief reasons why it is difficult to identify a scientific approach to teaching and learning that different cultural groups can agree on. The tradition of scientific management developed by Frederick W. Taylor and popularized in the early years of the twentieth century by educational reformers continues to reappear in different reincarnations, but its only benefit has been to those who have gained recognition through writing books and articles promoting the holy grail of increased efficiencies and measurable outcomes in educational performance.

Educational theorists' insistence that theories of learning meet the scientific criteria of objective measurement and replicability has led to a huge literature and endless hours of required courses in educational psychology. The different theories of learning these courses present, however, are all predicated on the assumption that intelligence is an attribute of the autonomous individual. The recent attention given to the ideas of Lev S. Vygotsky by prominent psychologists such as Jerome Bruner is one of the few encouraging developments in what has otherwise been a dismal record of achievement. It is important to note, however, that the reductionist science that has been the hallmark of mainstream educational psychology was not the primary influence on the development of Vygostky's thinking. Rather, it was his observations of the interconnections between language and cognition in social settings that opened the door to understanding the multiple ways in which the languaging processes of a cultural group carry forward the taken-for-granted thought patterns that are the basis of the group's form of intelligence.

Generations of educators have viewed science as providing objective data about the effectiveness of teaching and classroom management. They have used science to legitimate theories of learning with their roots in Western philosophic assumptions that would have been challenged if they were not so well hidden in the rhetoric of science—which the public has been educated to view as a nonpolitical mode of inquiry. As a number of recent educational critics—including McLaren, Giroux, and Apple—have observed, science-based approaches to educational reform invariably strengthen the social stratification patterns of the larger society and contribute to reducing the curriculum to learning tasks and information that can be "objectively measured." In effect, educational reformers' traditional reliance on the epistemology, research methodology, and metatheories of science has created schools that prepare a workforce that is largely unaware of its own cultural traditions. This "educated" workforce has not been taught to understand the deep cultural assumptions that have led to replacing the communal nature of work and the skilled worker with computer-driven machines. In effect, science-based approaches to educational reform have created a generation of rootless individuals easily shaped by the hundreds of thousands of media commercials that they encounter over a lifetime. Not even science-based environmental education classes teach students how the dominant cultural patterns of thinking contribute to the pollution of the local ecosystem they are studying.

Today the mechanistic sciences are being challenged by discoveries in fields ranging from quantum mechanics to the sciences of complexity, and a few educational reformers are attempting to explain how the goals of education and classroom practices can be aligned with these new areas of scientific inquiry. But before we take a look at these educational theorists and the implications of their work for an eco-justice pedagogy, we must first examine the proposals for educational reforms that are still based on mechanistic and highly reductionist approaches to the scientific study of the brain.

Educational Reforms Based on Brain Research

Reading about how educators propose to use brain research in the classroom is a disconcerting experience. They restate the explanations of brain activity found in the writings of Francis Crick, Antonio R. Damasio, and Paul and Patricia Churchland with a sense of absolute certainty that the electrochemical processes that transmit messages through various systems in the brain tell the entire story. Yet, buried near the end of the educational extrapolations from the "extra ordinary neural machine," as Crick puts it, the reader finds an admission that the actual causal relationships occurring in the brain are not fully known. Jane Healy, the author of *Endangered Minds: Why Children Don't Think and What We Can Do about It* (1990) and *Failure to Connect: How Computers Affect Our Children's Minds—for Better and Worse* (1998), acknowledges that "much of what we are learning now in the name of the brain is actually hypothetical, projected from the few things we know." She also observes that "brain research thus far has only given us a few clues, not prescriptions, about how we should raise our children and teach them" (1998:6).

In *A Celebration of Neurons: An Educator's Guide to the Human Brain* (1995), a monograph sponsored by the Association for Supervision and Curriculum Development, Robert Sylwester concludes his detailed summary of the development of the brain and how messages from external stimuli are distributed through the neural networks with an observation that should have appeared on the first page. "Current brain theory and research," he notes, "provides only the broad tantalizing outlines of what the school of the future should be." This admission does not dampen his optimism that brain research will determine the future direction of educational reform; it is merely that "educators who are willing to study the new cognitive science developments . . . will have to work out the specifics in the years ahead" (141).

Even Howard Gardner's theory of how the brain is "designed" to process eight distinct forms of intelligence, which some educators are embracing with the same certainty that they accord to the law of gravity, is based on basic uncertainties. Might there be a ninth or tenth form of intelligence, for instance, and is there a genetic basis for each form of intelligence? There is an even more important question that Gardner and his followers do not ask; namely, is individual intelligence largely encoded in the languaging patterns of the cultural group? If we consider the intelligence expressed in the dominant culture—from the design of houses, modes of transportation, and how disease is understood and treated to the primacy given to defining wealth in economic terms—it becomes difficult to grasp how intelligence can be understood as an attribute of the autonomous individual. Unfortunately, the daily reenactment of cultural patterns within a range of individualized interpretation that still allows for communication to be understood by others within the same epistemic/language community has not led to rethinking the twenty-five-hundred-year legacy of Western philosophy and the one-hundred-year legacy of psychology—and now brain research. Even though comparative studies of other cultures and of our own taken-for-granted epistemic patterns do not support it, the individual remains the focus of the experts' attention. I will return to a more careful examination of the cultural nature of intelligence as part of the discussion of how to practice an eco-justice pedagogy. For now, it is important to stay focused on how educational reforms are being extrapolated from the scientific study of the brain.

Classroom teachers across the country are attending workshops to learn how to match instruction with the stages of the brain's development. They are also learning about the connections between such behaviors as attention, emotional responses, and abstract thinking and the distributive characteristics of neural networks in the brain. They attend these workshops with the expectation that science is at last providing the basis for knowing which teaching strategy and curricular content will be most appropriate to their students' stage of development.

Robert Sylwester is perhaps the most widely traveled on this teacher workshop circuit. The combination of the highly technical vocabulary he uses to explain the workings of the brain with the teachers' lack of a scientific background that would enable them to assess both the accuracy of his explanation and when his extrapolations are unwarranted make for a questionable educational experience. As most teachers do not know what his explanations leave out (namely, that languaging reproduces the taken-for-granted cultural schemata that influence our patterns of thinking and expression), his representation of causal connections within the brain as scientific fact goes largely unchallenged. Witness his summary of "memory at the cellular and network levels":

> Memory networks form their chemical connections at the synapse, the narrow gap that neurotransmitters cross when they move from [the] axon terminal of a presynaptic neuron to attach to receptors on the dendrites or cell body of a postsynaptic neuron.
>
> When our sensory system focuses on an object or event, it activates a large number of neurons that are assembled in a variety of related brain networks (generally, combinations of columns). Each network processes a specific property of the object or event, such as its shape or movement pattern. This initial simultaneous activation creates synchronized response patterns in the coalition of activated neural

networks—principally in their firing rates and in the amounts of neurotransmitters their neurons release. This activity somehow links the networks that process various properties of the object or event, and we get a mental impression of spatial integration—for instance, we perceive a face as a unit—even though the various brain areas are operating independently, and no single brain site contains a total face. (Sylwester 1995:88–89)

Sylwester ends the paragraph with the statement that "scientists don't completely understand the process, but they believe that attention, thought, and memory emerge out of such synchronized patterns of neural network activity." It is doubtful that many classroom teachers have the courage to challenge Sylwester's explanation by drawing on personal experience in order to point out, for example, that meaning is integral to interpreting what is being communicated by another person's facial expressions. As meaning is at the center of metacommunication about relationships, and meaning is largely influenced by culture, the question becomes: Does Sylwester really think that the aesthetic judgment about another person's face, as well as the assessment of character and the interpretation of how the other's facial gestures metacommunicate about ongoing relationships—or even the memory of an earlier encounter with a similar facial expression—can be accounted for in terms of "synchronized patterns of neural networks"? When we read statements such as "our brain is not part of the external environment. Imprisoned and protected within the darkness and silence of our skull, it depends on its sensory and motor systems for external access," the answer appears to be "yes." When Sylwester gets around to mentioning cultural phenomena such as stereotypical thinking, he avoids explaining how it influences the electrochemical processes of the brain. The following quote reiterates a key point that he shares with theorists in the field of brain research. "Our brain," he says, "is not part of the external environment"; thus culture can be treated as an epiphenomenon—if it is mentioned at all.

Teachers who sit through his explanation of how emotions and other conscious processes are the result of neurotransmitters sending either "excitatory or inhibitory messages" to receiving neurons find the educational implications to be little more than the conventional wisdom they have already gained from their interactions with students. As I want to make explicit the ideology that is implicit in Sylwester's interpretation of the classroom implications of brain research, I will quote several of his educational recommendations. "The classrooms of the future," he suggests, "might focus more on drawing out existing abilities than on precisely measuring one's success with imposed skills, encourage the personal construction of categories rather than impose existing categorical systems, and emphasize the individual, personal solutions of an environmental challenge (even if inefficient) over the efficient group manipulation that merely represent the solution" (23). In the chapter titled "How Our Brain Determines What's Important," which explains various theories of how neural systems regulate emotions and attention, Sylwester recommends that "schools should focus more on metacognitive activities that encourage students to talk about their emotions, listen to the feeling of classmates, and to think about the motivations of people who enter their curricular world" (76). He also suggests that "two guiding principles of classroom management and instruction emerge out of our current knowledge about attention mechanisms and processes. First, teachers should adapt their instruction to the built-in biases of the students' stable (or innate) attentional mechanisms. Second, they should use imaginative teaching and management strategies to enhance the development of their students' adaptable attention processes" (82–83).

The problem with using the chemistry of the brain to establish a scientific basis for educational reform proposals that turn out to be little more than common sense is that it diverts attention away from the central challenge that many groups other than educators are recognizing. How do we change the formal and informal educational processes in ways that reinforce the values and patterns of consciousness that strengthen the interdependence of community and reduce the emphasis on consumerism and economic growth? Or, as Gregory Smith puts it, how do we teach learning to live within limits (1992)?

The effort to base educational reforms on the "objective findings" of science may appear to many educators, and even to the lay public, to be free of ideology and economic self-interest. That Sylwester's ideological orientation is also taken for granted by others whose thought processes are largely constituted by the same language that frames his interpretation of the educational implications of brain research adds to the perception that science is an objective and thus culturally neutral way of knowing. This myth is easily exposed by an examination of how his classroom proposals center on strengthening the autonomy of the individual. Teachers, he says, must "encourage the personal construction of categories," "emphasize the individual, personal solutions," and "encourage students to talk about their emotions." This emphasis on individuals constructing their own categories for the organization of knowledge is the ideal of a modern way of thinking; it is *not* found in cultures that have not yet been overwhelmed by the cultural messages of the Western media and technological fundamentalism. As I explained earlier, this view of individualism is predicated on other culturally specific assumptions: most notably, the assumptions that constant change is the expression of progress, that humans need to bring the environment under rational control, and that the modern form of consciousness is more evolutionarily advanced.

In addition to the ideology reflected in his educational recommendations, Sylwester's effort to base educational decisions on neurophysiological research reinforces other Western cultural patterns that raise important moral questions and are profoundly political in nature. While the attempt of Sylwester and other like-minded educators to align educational reforms with the findings of brain research is well intentioned, they are nevertheless reinforcing a way of thinking that uncritically looks to science for answers to how to control student behavior and learning. This leads, by extension, to an increasing dependence on psychiatrists, cognitive scientists, and drug company chemists to define what constitutes normal behavior. The slippery slope these scientists have put us on can be seen in the routine use of mind-altering drugs in schools to control student behavior.

Allowing scientists to define what constitutes normal behavior and the nature of consciousness has the effect of relegating culture to the junk heap of prescientific thinking. All things considered, the use of Prozac and Ritalin to control students is a minor moral issue compared with scientists' attempts to alter the genetic codes that direct the development of cells and organs and to clone animals—with the next step being the cloning of humans. There is even an effort to develop protein-based computers that will become, as Joel Birnbaum (the director of the Hewlett-Packard Laboratories) prophesied at a recent computer conference held in San Jose, California, auxiliary brains.

In 1967, Marshall Nirenberg (who received the Nobel Prize for his work on the language of the genetic code) expressed his concern with scientists' lack of preparation for addressing the moral issues looming in the future of scientific research. In an article that appeared in *Science,* he shared his deepest concern: "My guess is that cells will be programmed with synthetic messages within 25 years. . . . The point that deserves special emphasis is that man may be able to program his own cells long before he will be able to assess adequately the long-term consequences of such alterations, long before he will be able to formulate goals, and long before he can resolve the ethical and moral problems which will be raised" (1967:157). He could have stated the problem more directly by pointing out that the scientific method and its legitimating ideology, which is based on the same Western myths that underpin modern consciousness, have no self-limiting moral principles. That is, there is no domain of existence that is considered sacred and thus off-limits to scientific inquiry. Whatever the cultural/personal moral norms of individual scientists, they are easily abridged by the allure of financial gain from patents and the need to pursue a line of research in order to obtain the publications required for professional advancement. Perhaps the greatest motivation for ignoring the moral codes of a cultural group and the dangers of introducing a potentially harmful synthetic chemical or microorganism into the environment is the desire to attain a kind of immortality by becoming the discoverer of a new natural phenomenon or research technique.

For examples of how easily the scientist's moral principles can be discarded for purposes of economic gain we need look no further than a recent genetic engineering project being carried out by scientists working for a subsidiary of Monsanto that focuses its research program on industrializing the world's food supply. The project was recently shelved in response to widespread public protest. The new plant they were designing, for which a patent was to be sought in eighty-seven countries, was genetically altered to enhance crop yield and to release a toxin that would cross-pollinate with nearby crops. The toxin would strip the other plants of their ability to produce viable seeds, forcing farmers to purchase seeds for the next year's planting rather than saving the best of their own seeds for that purpose. Monsanto would have reaped immense profits had this plant been sold in its intended market: the agriculturally stressed regions of the world. But the estimated $1.5 billion per year profit would have come at the expense of those least able to afford the cost. It is important to emphasize that it was the public rather than the scientific community that forced Monsanto to drop the "terminator" seed project.

And this is the mode of inquiry that Sylwester and other educators want to make the basis of teacher decision making! The advocates of brain-based educational reforms look at one side of the Janus face of science and see only constructive achievements. They do not acknowledge the social and ecological injustices it engenders. They do not question the increasing use of drugs to control student behavior—one of the outcomes of brain research—or challenge the view of intelligence being promoted by scientists who view the brain as a computer. Even more important, these educators ignore the eco-justice issues that arise from scientific experiments that begin in the lab, move into the industrial process of mass production and dissemination, and complete the cycle by undermining the chemistry that sustains the self-renewing capacity of natural systems. Their failure to place the achievements and failures of scientific research within the broader context of a multicultural world, with its differing moral codes and ways of knowing, further undermines the ability of teachers, parents, and the general public to challenge the tunnel vision of scientists.

Educational Reforms Based on Chaos Theory and Whitehead's Cosmology

Modern science no longer measures and explains the world in terms of cause-and-effect relationships. According to the current view, the interaction of systems with other systems introduces disequilibrium (chaos, disorder) out of which new patterns of order emerge. This trend has not gone unnoticed by educational theorists, who have discovered an apparent correspondence between Alfred N. Whitehead's cosmology, which represents all forms of being as inseparable from "becoming," and nonlinear dynamics. Indeed, the new discoveries in chaos theory and the revival of interest in the ideas of Whitehead have added an unaccustomed vigor to the Deweyian tradition of educational reform. At last, science promises to provide a basis for reforming education in ways that will bring everyday experiences in line with the complex and dynamic patterns occurring in the natural world.

This current effort to model the educational process on the characteristics of nonlinear dynamic systems seems likely to replace the grand scientific theory that propelled the Industrial Revolution with another grand theory. The eco-justice issues of this development are especially important because this new grand theory can easily be extended to explain how the cultural disruptions caused by the globalization of Western technology and consumerism become the wellspring for new nonlinear patterns of self-organization within the world's cultures.

The basic conceptual problems connected with this new approach to using education to reform the cultures of the world are best explained through an analysis of the writings of William E. Doll Jr. and Donald Oliver, the most prominent advocates of the "postmodern" paradigm shift in educational reform. Because Doll chiefly draws on Ilya Prigogine and Isabelle Stengers's book, *Order out of Chaos: Man's New Dialogue with Nature* (1984), and Oliver's thinking represents an extension of Whitehead's process philosophy, my analysis will not address the arguments within the scientific community surrounding Prigogine's extrapolations from the theory of chaotic systems. It should also be kept in mind that other educational theorists, as well as organizational change theorists such as Margaret J. Wheatly, are fostering a wider interest in the ideas of Prigogine and Whitehead. Journal articles as well as papers presented at educational conferences with titles such as "Cognition, Complexity, and Teacher Education," "A Review of Basic Principles of Catastrophe Theory and Their Application to Learning and Development," and "Complexity Theory for Classroom Management" represent a growing interest in the classroom implications of what appears to have the authority of cutting-edge scientific research. There is even a Chaos and Complexity Theory interest group that holds its yearly meeting under the auspices of the American Educational Research Association and supports a web page designed to internationalize this new genre of educational reform.

Doll uses the categories of open and closed systems as a conceptual framework to set chaos theory and Whitehead's process philosophy off from what he refers to as the paradigm of modernism. Closed systems, which Doll associates with modernism, are based on the mechanistic sciences of Newton and the bifurcated world and instrumental thinking of Descartes. This view of the universe as fixed and measurable led, as Doll puts it, to "the concept of curriculum as autonomous but interconnected units. . . . From the first grade on, curriculum is considered in terms of units arranged in a linear order" (1993:38). The difference, as he sums it up, is that "closed systems transmit and transfer; open systems transform" (57).

He goes on to explain his objection to "closed systems" in the following way:

> For the most part modernist curriculum thought has adopted the closed version, one where—through focusing—knowledge is transmitted, transferred. This is, I believe, what our best contemporary schooling is about. Transmission frames our teaching-learning process. We define good teaching (resulting in good learning) as the transfer of knowledge—often in the form of noble works and accepted procedures of the Western, humanist tradition. Until now,

the thermodynamic concept of an open system—one that transforms through dissipation—has not been explored for curriculum considerations. (58)

This brings us to the question of what Doll means by the "thermodynamic concept of an open system." And that is where Prigogine's Nobel Prize–winning study of "dissipative structures" becomes relevant.

Prigogine sums up an essential feature of thermodynamic systems as follows: "At all levels, be it the level of macroscopic physics, the level of fluctuations, or the microscopic level, nonequilibrium is the source of order. Nonequilibrium brings 'order out of chaos'" (Prigogine and Stengers 1984:286–287). Systems representing different scales of existence fluctuate in ways that may set off internal changes or changes in adjoining systems. What Prigogine calls the "bifurcation point" occurs at the moment a system moves into a state of disequilibrium and nonlinear relationship with previous patterns. At this point it also becomes impossible to predict the new form of order and complexity that will emerge from this condition of "chaos." As Prigogine's research has shown, the formation of this new dynamic state leads to increased differentiation and complexity—or what he calls a dissipative structure. Doll and the other educational theorists interested in the classroom implications of chaos theory hold that cultural systems behave in the same way. That is, out of chaos (disruption in cultural patterns caused by internal or external forces) emerges a higher level of order that will, in turn, involve a new bifurcation point that moves the system to a new and unpredictable level of complexity and order, and so on.

Prigogine's theory, which has been validated through a number of scientific experiments, contradicts the second law of thermodynamics, which holds that changes in natural systems lead to the dissipation of energy. In effect, it represents the biosphere and the microscopic world as evolving in the direction of increased differentiation and complexity. This science of process and increased complexity (progress) provides Doll and his co-theorists with the scientific evidence on which to base an approach to teaching and learning that avoids "transmitting" knowledge and values from one generation to the next. Furthermore, because the theory of dissipative structures is interpreted as explaining the behavior of systems in both the physical world and the social world, Doll and his co-theorists represent their reform proposals as having universal applicability. That is, they are to be the basis of educational reform in cultures as diverse as those found in China, India, Africa, the Middle East, and across North and South America. These educational recommendations are buttressed by the group's acceptance of Whitehead's philosophical ideas, which share two theses with Prigogine's theory: (1) reality is characterized by the continual emergence of more complex forms of existence, and (2) the theory does not have to be qualified to take account of differences in cultural ways of knowing. As Doll has written the most comprehensively on the educational implications of Prigogine's theory, I focus on his ideas rather than those of his co-theorists, who are mainly backfilling and making minor extensions.

Doll states the main implication of Prigogine's theory in the following way:

> What seems characteristic of all self-organizing patterns is that they
> occur when "a critical threshold is reached," whereupon atoms, cells,
> or other entities "suddenly organize themselves on a global scale and
> execute cooperative behavior." . . . . Such a statement has powerful
> curricular as well as cosmological implications. One curriculum
> implication is that if cooperative, purposeful behavior (which leads to
> higher levels of organization) suddenly appears at critical threshold
> points, then teachers need to work toward finding these junctions in

their own group interactions. And if autocatalysm and iteration take over at some point, so that a given class generates its own order and methods of development, then finding these junctions might well be one of the most important tasks a teacher has. (1993:104–105)

Doll further suggests that a postmodern pedagogy will emerge from the "concept of self-organization," and this process should dictate the role of the teacher. As he explains: "one requirement is perturbation. A system self-organizes only when there is perturbation, problem, or disturbance—when the system is unsettled and needs to resettle, to continue functioning" (163). Thus, the teacher's role is to be a catalyst who introduces the disequilibrium that triggers a new level of self-organization. The teacher carries out this role, as other progressive educators have argued over the last one hundred years, by providing a learning environment "rich enough and open enough for multiple uses, interpretations, and perspectives to come into play" (164). As Doll is aware that an "open system" approach to education can easily foster the idea that everything may become relative to the perspective of the student, he adds at the end of his explanation of the teacher as "first among equals" four guidelines for avoiding a descent into nihilism. These pedagogical and curricular guidelines include ensuring that the curriculum involves richness, recursion, relations, and rigor—which suggests that the teacher is not to rely entirely on the spontaneous self-organization of chaotic systems in the classroom.

Even someone with only a casual understanding of the history of progressive education—one that encompasses the ideas of the early reformers who integrated the ideas of Rousseau, Freud, and Dewey into those of the later neoromantics such as Carl Rogers—cannot fail to recognize that Doll's attempt to base educational reform on the science of complex systems leads to essentially the same view of education held by these earlier progressive thinkers. While Doll claims that modern education was based on the mechanistic paradigm (exemplified in the thinking of Ralph Tyler and Madeline Hunter), he fails to acknowledge that his own recommendations are essentially a restatement of the progressive vision of education as process, exploration, and growth. He also fails to recognize that the "closed system" of modernism is actually a gross misrepresentation—even of the sciences on which the earlier phase of the Industrial Revolution was based.

The deep cultural assumptions guiding the social uses of the mechanistic sciences emphasized the connection between change and progress, the autonomous nature of the rational individual, the extension of the commodification process into all areas of knowledge and relationships, and the pursuit of new technologies that would facilitate the further control and exploitation of the natural world. Modernity can be viewed as based on a mechanistic paradigm only if one is highly selective of the evidence—such as citing specific traditions in medicine, architecture, education, brain research, and so forth. But even when the mechanistic root metaphor led to the use of a mechanistic language and thought process, as in the Bauhaus school of architecture and current brain research, the emphasis was always on fostering innovation and change. In effect, the expression of mechanistic thinking was directed toward overturning the traditions of cultural groups who otherwise would have resisted being integrated into the growth-oriented economic and technological system. The "perturbations" introduced into traditional cultures by the early phase of the Industrial Revolution were viewed by these supposed "closed system" thinkers as leading to a point of disequilibrium that would result in the emergence of a higher form of complexity (i.e., progress). A strong case can even be made that the cultural assumptions that gave conceptual and moral direction to modernism are still taken for granted by most scientists who are attempting to translate their understanding of the behavior of complex systems into new technologies.

Doll's distinction between closed systems (modernism) and open systems (postmodernism) holds up only if one ignores the dominant characteristics of capitalism, the ideology of academic institutions (including the sciences), the relentless drive within the arts to find new forms of expression, and the characteristics of populist democracy. The search for new ideas, values, technologies, and personal identities and economic opportunities has long been at the core of high-status institutions and social groups bent on modernizing different segments of the multidimensional Western culture. This same messianic impulse—as well as the profit motive and desire for power—is at the center of current efforts by multinational corporations to create a worldwide monoculture.

There are, however, more serious problems connected with the use of science as a basis for reforming education. They show up in particularly blatant form when Doll extends Prigogine's theory of dissipative structures into a general theory of how to turn the world's cultures into spontaneously self-organizing systems. I say "world's cultures" because Doll, like the critical pedagogy theorists, universalizes his prescriptions. The most fundamental error that Doll and like-minded educational theorists make is in treating cultural and natural phenomena as behaving in the same way. Even if we grant that perturbations in natural systems lead to new patterns of differentiation and complexity, from a cultural point of view the new level of self-organization does not always reduce human suffering and turmoil.

First, there is danger in assuming that the characteristics of self-organization observed in natural systems are the same characteristics operating in cultures that differ widely in how they reproduce the symbol systems essential to their identity, forms of storage and renewal, and patterns of interaction and moral reciprocity. The perturbation caused when the first slave ships appeared off the coast of West Africa, for example, led to new patterns of self-organization among both the slave owners and the slaves. But the new level of differentiation and complexity, which I read Doll as equating with progress, contributed to the moral equivalent of the second law of thermodynamics. That is, this complex set of perturbations degraded everyone involved—but in different ways. Furthermore, as Doll tends to view the old patterns in a negative light, a case can be made that slaves' efforts to keep alive vernacular traditions essential to maintaining family and community networks of support were an expression of strength in the face of the constant threat that their owners would introduce further perturbations into their lives. Other instances in which the old patterns became sources of resistance to dissipative structures that were far more oppressive than the patterns they replaced are numerous; the gun, gas chamber, and gulag are examples of destructive perturbations.

Second, we can consider other examples of "bifurcation points" (to use Prigogine's vocabulary) that introduced disequilibrium by asking whether a higher level of order or dissipative structure emerged. Did a higher level of order emerge, for example, from the assassination of Archduke Francis Ferdinand by Gravrilo Princeps; from dropping the atom bomb on Hiroshima; from mining uranium on the Navajo Reservation; or from introducing genetically engineered seeds resistant to herbicides that allow farmers to destroy "weeds" (the surrounding ground cover), and thus reduce plant diversity, without harming their crops? The number of dissipative structures emerging from the perturbations of power, greed, and simple miscalculation are nearly endless—and while they could be described as more complex, they cannot always be viewed in the progressive light that fits Doll's interpretation.

The problem goes deeper than the inadequacy of Prigogine's metaphors, which are particularly problematic when they are used to account for the impact of cultural practices on natural systems. For example, the use of new technologies in the fishing industry introduced a condition of disequilibrium in the marine ecosystem in the coastal waters of the maritime provinces and states. The over-fishing of cod precipitated a rapid decline in their numbers to the point where scientists questioned the ability of the species to recover. The niche vacated by the cod was filled by other species less useful to humans as a source of protein. The metaphors *order out of chaos, becoming, arrow of time,* and *open systems that evolve to higher and higher forms of complexity* (all metaphors used by Prigogine) tend to legitimate the Western myth that change is directional and inherently progressive in nature. A careful reading of Doll's writings, as well as those of other educational theorists similarly influenced by chaos theory, suggests that their interpretation of the science of complexity simply reinforces a proclivity of modern thinkers to ignore cultural and environmental changes that challenge the myth of progress.

One further point must be made about the danger of borrowing from a scientific theory that supports the assumptions on which the continuing Industrial Revolution is based. Both Prigogine and Doll explain change as evolving toward increased complexity. And, indeed, if we examine how the introduction of modern technologies changed indigenous cultures, we find new forms of complexity—in legal systems, police functions, bureaucratic control, missionary work, and other apparatus of the modern state necessary for the education of a workforce, the expansion of markets, and welfare programs. The new forms of complexity have bound indigenous cultures into webs of dependence within a colonial system. At the same time, the forms of complexity associated with intergenerational knowledge about ceremonies and technologies attuned to the characteristics of the bioregion—such as herbal medicines and narratives that encoded the moral templates governing relationships—were undermined. This replacement of traditions of self-sufficiency by the modern "antitraditions" that turn relationships into commodities, which in turn creates poverty and unemployment, have been well documented by Helena Norberg-Hodge, Frédérique Apffel-Marglin, and Vandana Shiva.

The resistance of farmers in India to the introduction of genetically engineered seeds and the efforts of the indigenous cultures in the Andes to regenerate their ancient traditions of agriculture and ceremony provide a different perspective on the arrow of change that Prigogine and Doll interpret as always leading away from the past and toward "higher and higher levels of complexity." As I pointed out earlier, the ancient cosmology that governed the Andean cultures' approach to agriculture resulted in a genetic diversity of edible plants unmatched in human history. Instead of the arrow of change moving in the direction of more complex and differentiated systems, as Prigogine and Doll hold, the modern laboratory approach to agriculture has led to reduced genetic diversity. Is this progress?

Because educational theorists view Whitehead's philosophy as further justification for basing educational reform on an "open system," I will make a few observations about the eco-justice implications of relying on Whitehead for guidance on the role of education in effecting the renewal of the world's cultures. Donald Oliver has established himself as the most comprehensive interpreter of the educational significance of Whitehead's ideas, and I focus here primarily on his extrapolations. In assessing the form of cultural renewal that Oliver views as being consistent with Whitehead's process philosophy it is important to remember that Whitehead collaborated with Bertrand Russell in writing *Principia Mathematica*, and also that his philosophical writings, including *Process and Reality*, were not based on a comparative understanding of cultural ways of knowing. Indeed, Whitehead wrote in the style that has been a hallmark of Western philosophers in which words are taken to have universal meanings.

Whitehead's early interest in mathematics and failure to consider the multiplicity of cultural ways of knowing fail to make educational theorists such as Oliver cautious about making his ideas the conceptual linchpin of educational reform. Indeed, these limitations are not even mentioned in Oliver's writings. Whitehead's ideas, as interpreted by Oliver and other educational theorists, including Doll, are being interpreted as giving philosophical support to recent scientific discoveries about the behavior of complex systems. It is to Oliver's credit that in framing the educational significance of Whitehead's thinking he develops an insightful critique of the distortions caused by modernity. He also gives extended treatment to the connections between modernity and the ecological crisis. These concerns, however, do not lead to a recognition of the ways Whitehead's process philosophy actually supports the deepest symbolic foundations of modernity—and thus a form of culture that is having a devastating impact on the environment and the diversity of the world's cultures.

A few key ideas of this mathematician-turned-philosopher will serve as reference points for understanding the context-free nature of his arguments—that is, how he represents reality as if it were the same for all cultures. For example, Whitehead explains the nature of knowledge in the following way: "All knowledge is conscious discrimination of objects experienced. But this conscious discrimination, which is knowledge, is nothing more than an additional factor in the subjective interplay of subject with object. This interplay is the stuff constituting those individual things which make up the sole reality of the Universe. These individual things are the individual occasions of experience, the actual entities. . . . And all knowledge is derived from, and verified by, direct intuitive observation" (Whitehead 1953:800). As Edward Sapir's pioneering work in clarifying how languaging carries forward a cultural group's way of knowing was not then widely recognized, it is not surprising that Whitehead's contemporaries accepted his explanation of knowledge. With the number of books that now exist on the metaphorical nature of the language-thought connection (which both supports Sapir's basic insights and explains one of the characteristics of linguistic change), however, it is more difficult to understand how that could be the case today. The basic problem with Whitehead's understanding of knowledge as the subjective interplay of objects and events in the natural world is that it ignores that the individual's interpretation and behavior are largely influenced by cultural schemata acquired in the process of learning the language systems of the cultural group. Thus it ignores that the subjective, what Whitehead refers to as the "direct intuitive observation," is largely influenced by cultural assumptions and categories of thinking that are, for the most part, taken for granted in the acts of perception, interpretation, and behavior.

Whitehead's view of change as moving forward is equally uninformed by an awareness of how different cultures interpret the nature of time. The following statement by Whitehead supports both Prigogine's view of time as like an arrow moving forward and Doll's equation of change with progress. Its Western origins are obvious if we consider the way time is conceptualized and experienced in indigenous cultures of North and South America, the Indian subcontinent, China, Japan, and Southeast Asia. Whitehead, who universalizes time in a way that makes "becoming" an essential quality of being, posits that:

> we essentially perceive our relations with nature because they are in the making. The sense of action is that essential factor in natural knowledge which exhibits it as a self-knowledge enjoyed by an element of nature respecting its active relations with the whole of nature in its various aspects. Natural knowledge is merely the other side of action. The *forward moving time* exhibits this characteristic of experience, that it is essentially action. This passage of nature—or, in

other words, *its creative advance*—is its fundamental characteristic; the traditional concept is an attempt to catch nature without its passage. (1953:168; italics added)

And in another statement that anticipates Prigogine's extrapolations from the study of nonlinear phenomena that represent disorder as the spontaneous source of an emergent and more complex form of order, Whitehead writes: "The distinction between 'appearance' and 'reality' is grounded in the process of self-formation of each actual occasion. The objective content of the initial phase of reception is the real antecedent world, as given for that occasion. This is the 'reality' from which that creative advance starts. It is the basic fact of the new occasion, with its concordances and discordances awaiting coordination in the new creature" (1953:830). Oliver and his collaborator, Kathleen Waldron Gershman, do express their concern about the destructive impact of modern consciousness on the Earth's ecosystems. Nevertheless, their book, *Education, Modernity, and Fractured Meaning: Toward a Process Theory of Teaching and Learning* (1989), focuses on the classroom implications of Whitehead's cosmology. And it is Whitehead's explanation of concrescence that becomes the central feature of Oliver's educational reform proposals.

"Concrescence," Oliver explains, "means having become something novel as a result of a unifying of diverse elements" (1989:117). The rest of Oliver's explanation holds the key to the role he thinks teachers should play in the process of "becoming," as students, teacher, and the environment interact with each other. Especially noteworthy is Oliver's insistence that the process of becoming does not involve the influence of cultural patterns. He explains that becoming, "is impelled from within; coming from within, it has its own motive, its ideal of itself; its subjective aim" (117). Furthermore, the "prehension" of the students, teacher, and aspects of the natural world that constitute the curriculum, which Whitehead defines as "feeling," is not to be distracted or repressed by a curriculum that has been determined in advance.

Thus, teaching and learning as a process of becoming involve the joint construction of new understandings, values, and patterns of interaction—which are in harmony with the basic processes governing the universe. As Oliver puts it:

> Process teaching . . . begins by assuming that teacher, student, curriculum, materials (books, crayons, paper, etc.) are all moving in a novel occasion. We do not begin from a special position of nothing (before the class begins) to "making something happen." Teacher and student are constantly in the flow of occasions as they move toward fulfillment, are transformed, perish, and become part of another occasion. The major thrust of planning for the teacher is to imagine what circumstances might move the occasion of potentiality into concrescence. The teacher sees himself or herself as moving within time in the midst of a happening, in the midst of emerging pattern. . . . The teacher does not move forward to cause something to happen; the teacher moves when there is a good feeling, when things feel right. (1989:162–163)

Oliver's reliance on Whitehead's process view of reality is supported by the same cultural assumptions that lead Doll to use Prigogine's theory of dissipative structures as the basis of curricular reform. Ironically, neither Oliver nor Doll appears to recognize that what they accept as a description of the creative unfolding of reality is in actuality a modern/postmodern interpretation of culture's progress over generations of encountering internal and external forces.

Oliver and Doll share a number of fundamental misunderstandings with earlier process-oriented educational reformers such as A. S. Neill, Carl Rogers, and John Dewey. First, they assume that the educational process should free individuals from cultural patterns that limit the spontaneous process of self-organization. It is important to note that they do not take the position, as I have done, that destructive traditions need to be made explicit and transformed while traditions that contribute to the moral coherence and ecological sustainability of communities need to be renewed and preserved. Indeed, their way of representing modern education as a process in which knowledge is "transmitted, transferred," to use Doll's characterization (and which Oliver describes as "transferring a piece of knowledge"), reflects the same dichotomous thinking that led Paulo Freire to claim that his method of consciousness raising represents the alternative to the "banking approach" to education.

Second, their distinction between "transferring" and "creating" knowledge distorts the multiple ways in which intergenerational learning occurs. It also grossly misrepresents the multiple ways learning occurs in classrooms not organized around the principles of scientific management or run by authoritarian and ressentient teachers. More important, their lack of understanding of the different ways that cultural patterns are learned at a taken-for-granted level prevents them from developing a theory of education that takes into account the teacher's responsibility in mediating the students' encounter with their own culture's symbolic world and the deeply held assumptions encoded in the thinking and technologies of other cultural groups. For example, if Doll and Oliver had understood that their representation of what constitutes an authentic, creative, transformative educational experience would be interpreted in terms of taken-for-granted cultural assumptions about the progressive nature of change, they might have included in their theory of education a more complex understanding of how the languaging processes that sustain everyday life encode cultural intelligence.

Third, their representation of education as an unfolding process centered on the immediacy of the student-teacher relationship fails to address eco-justice issues that vary from culture to culture. Both Oliver and Doll acknowledge the importance of the environment, but it is more a matter of genuflecting in the direction of what has become a god-word used in too many instances to legitimize the expansion of a consumer-oriented lifestyle. The ritual use of the term can be seen in the fact that their theories do not include a curriculum for studying the patterns of ecologically sustainable cultures and teaching students how to recognize and participate in the noncommodified activities of their own communities.

Fourth, their emphasis on the immediate transformative experience of the students and teacher and their corresponding warnings against a structured curriculum are unlikely to produce students with the background knowledge necessary to address eco-justice issues such as the systemic causes of racial and gender discrimination and the myriad cultural transformations wrought by the culture of cyberspace. This knowledge is unlikely to be acquired when the curriculum is organized in a way that causes "something (not determined in advance) to happen" (Oliver), and when the teacher is viewed as "first among equals" (Doll).

A historical perspective helps to elucidate the limitations of a process-centered approach to education. The child-centered phase of the earlier progressive education movement and the open classroom advocated by A. S. Neill and Carl Rogers did not produce students who were aware of patriarchy, racism, and the environmental and tradition-destroying effects of technology. And the constructivist approach being recycled today as the latest educational fad exhibits the same double bind in which the systematic examination of these issues would appear to violate the student's own construction of knowledge and growth toward greater autonomy. If these eco-justice issues became part of the curriculum, it was because the teachers were well-read political activists who were influenced by the explanations of relationships and historical developments that were part of their graduate education. Furthermore, these teachers organized what they taught about eco-justice in ways that connected with the lives of the students—which involved taking into account the cultural ecologies that influence the thought patterns and moral values of the students. If students learned about how they were embedded in and dependent on their bioregion, it was because older people in the community were brought into the educational process. Students are unlikely to learn about the multiple dimensions of work—which include combining the development of personal skills, craft knowledge learned in a mentoring relationship, and contributing something useful to the community—through self-discovery or their teacher's imagination of what might "move an occasion from potentiality into concrescence" (the word Whitehead uses to describe the "growing together" in a new complex unity).

It is doubtful that the process-oriented education proposed by Doll and Oliver would do more than represent a "time out" from the pressures of the modern culture. More likely, it would reinforce a rootless form of subjectivity in which the feelings connected with the immediate moment become the primary concern. This subjectively centered form of individualism also happens to be more easily manipulated by the media/business orientation that emphasizes the coemergence of change, progress, and happiness—and promotes freedom from the constraints of tradition.

A curriculum that borrows from chaos theory and an abstract cosmology that is intended to free us from lives based on earlier philosophically derived abstractions raises a number of eco-justice

issues. In assessing whether the theories of Prigogine and Whitehead can become the basis of an eco-justice pedagogy it is important to understand that neither understands how the complex symbolic systems of different cultures have influenced the adaptation of
technologies to the characteristics of the local environment. Nor do
they understand the development of cultural patterns that expand
aesthetic awareness, embody learning, and teach the role of narrative in renewing the moral codes governing relationships. While the
latter do not always meet today's moral standards in certain types
of relationships, they are vital to the interwoven patterns that connect generations, the collective experience of place, and the need
for symbolic renewal that are central features of communities—as
opposed to a society of individuals. Whitehead, for example, writes
as though his special vocabulary—*concrescence, prehension, ingres-
sion, event, creativity* (the latter he describes as the "universal of
universals")—has universal explanatory power. Prigogine's extrapolations end with a series of generalizations that restate the
modern hopes and concerns about the future as though they were
shared by all of the world's cultures. For example, he concludes
Order out of Chaos with a quotation from a Talmudic text that represents God as saying, "Let's hope 'it works.'" The text goes on to
observe that "this hope about the prospect of mankind is branded
with the mark of radical uncertainty" (Prigogine and Stengers
1984:313). This acknowledgment of uncertainty about the future,
which appears in the last paragraph of the book, has a certain
disingenuous ring. Like Whitehead, Prigogine makes no effort to
explain how his theory, when extended into the area of culture, can
be reconciled with the increased violence worldwide resulting from
the development of military technology, the colonization of non-
Western cultures through forced adoption of the Western model of
economic development, and the impact of high-status knowledge
promoted in Western universities on the moral fabric and local

economies of non-Western cultures. Given the failure of Whitehead and Prigogine to address these and other trends that have accelerated over the past decades, why do educational theorists look to them for conceptual and moral guidance? The only answer I can give is that the myth of progress is so deeply and unconsciously held that it leads to a case of highly selective perception of what is happening in the world.

The failure of Whitehead and Prigogine (as well as Dewey and other process thinkers) to understand the profound differences in cultural ways of knowing is reproduced in the educational proposals of Doll and Oliver. The varying degrees of syncretism of cultural groups within American society has not led to the disappearance of a sense of personal identity rooted in a distinct cultural heritage. Nor have the transforming pressures of the dominant culture eliminated the desire of parents, particularly those who take their intergenerational responsibility seriously, to ensure that the educational experiences of their children do not alienate them entirely from the traditions that are meaningful to the parents. Parents in the modern/postmodern tradition of thought expect that their children will be encouraged to experiment with new values and ideas, and that there will be a generation gap that reflects the differences in the technology that parents and child were initially socialized to interact with. Even parents holding fundamentalist values expect their children to interpret their world in ways that reflect generational differences—while continuing to embrace the core traditions they were raised with. If Doll and Oliver were to explain to parents that their children would experience a process-oriented education in which all traditions (beliefs, values, technologies, narratives, reciprocal moral norms, etc.) would be set aside in order to avoid obstructing the new form of order arising out of the immediate experience of the teacher and students, most parents would interpret that as a dangerous mix of nihilism and romanticism. Not even Doll's emphasis on a curriculum characterized by richness, recursion, relations, and rigor would lead them to accept the principle of self-organization as the central feature of the educational process. Indeed, his assertion that such a curriculum "becomes exciting, and engaging as it spirals off into the unknown" (Doll 1993:102) is more likely to deepen their concerns—especially if they value their ethnic heritage.

In effect, the Doll-Oliver process-based education is based on a new paradigm—one that no culture in the history of humankind has experienced. There is no evidence to support their implied claims that if people could make their lives accord with the principle of self-organization at the center of this new paradigm, injustice would be eliminated. Yet, they propose that parents surrender their voice in their children's education and adopt this new paradigm. That parental responsibility is being increasingly abrogated anyway for reasons connected with the need to spend more hours working in order to purchase what previously was produced within the home and community is not the issue here. Even if it were, the nihilism that is masked by the language of "process," "creativity," "open system," and so forth would not be able to compensate for the lack of responsible parenting. How to participate in a morally coherent community and engage in activities that have a smaller ecological footprint are, in part, learned through mentoring— which Doll and Oliver categorize as "transferring" knowledge and thus as the opposite of a transforming educational experience. We see here the limitations of their dichotomous categories, which in the above example do not acknowledge that mentoring is a matter of both transferring and transforming.

My other major concerns have already been alluded to, but they can be summarized in a way that highlights how the process approach to teaching and learning cannot address the systemic causes of the crises we face in our cultural and natural ecologies. Both Doll and Oliver, as well as the other educational theorists influenced by Whitehead and Prigogine, assume that the more unstructured a learning situation, the more creativity and self-organization will occur between students and the teacher—and thus the more positive the learning experience. Like Dewey, they view change as evolutionary and as leading to more complex and better-adapted responses to the ever-changing relationships that make up the environment. That an educational experience should always be a "novel occasion" (Oliver) and be governed by the "indeterminacy inherent in complexity and multiple perspectives" (Doll) means that it should always be an experiment with the symbolic foundations of the cultures represented in the classroom. This addiction to what is novel and experimental is a characteristic of many Western theorists and contains several double binds that deserve our consideration.

First, the assumption of progress, along with the idea of an emergent curriculum (with the teacher playing the role of facilitator), will contribute to a basic misunderstanding on the students' part. The chaos and disequilibrium students are taught to view as the necessary prelude to the progressive emergence of new patterns in the classroom are reinforced by the media's representation of new technologies and consumer necessities. This view of change will in turn reinforce the assumption that disorder and chaos in different sectors of society are part of the dialectic of progress. Following this line of thinking, the myriad forms of disorder in the world today— illnesses caused by chemical contaminants in the environment, the extreme weather patterns caused by changes in the carbon cycle, the growing impoverishment resulting from new technologies and the loss of intergenerational sharing of skills and knowledge— can be viewed as a natural part of the self-organization process that leads inevitably to a new and higher form of complexity. If disorder and chaos within systems lead to a more complex level of self-organization, why should students be concerned about anything beyond their own experiences of self-transformation? Students might even get the idea that contributing to disorder in cultural and natural systems is consistent with the internal logic of how nature works.

The other double bind relates to the need to recover cultural networks of mutual aid and solidarity overwhelmed by the Industrial Revolution. Forms of intergenerational knowledge essential to non-market-oriented relationships—narratives that carry forward knowledge of place and communal traditions, the skills that contribute to greater self-sufficiency of families and communities, knowledge of healing and ceremonies—are ideologically incompatible with a process-oriented curriculum. This system would not encourage students to examine how high-status knowledge leads to the introduction of technologies that create new forms of economic dependency. Nor would students encounter a curriculum that helps them recognize the many forms of face-to-face community that represent alternatives to finding community in the shopping mall, in cyberspace, and in the media. It is in these areas of daily life that eco-justice issues have direct implications for how we think about educational reform.

Basing Educational Reform on the Theory of Evolution

Charles Darwin's theory of evolution has become a modern metanarrative that is spreading unevenly through the strata of the world's cultures. It is filtering from the top downward and is complementing other metanarratives that justify the spread of the Western approach to economic and technological development. Although scientists themselves still disagree on minor and major aspects of the theory's explanatory power, academic disciplines such as psychology, anthropology, literature, and the fine arts are either adopting it as a basic conceptual framework or using its vocabulary to represent the dynamics of change and the functional nature of behaviors and individual attributes. Computer proponents find that placing developments in the computer industry within the context of natural selection and adaptation gives their business ethos of "survival of the fittest" the legitimacy of a law of nature. Even lawyers and judges are beginning to interpret antisocial behavior as accountable, in part, to the individual's genetic and thus evolutionary history.

Individuals educated to think in the categories of high-status knowledge view evolution and progress as nearly equivalent in meaning. They further assume that modern, literate cultures are more "evolved," and thus more complex and better adapted than traditional and largely oral cultures. But the majority of the world's cultures have encountered evolution only as a conceptual and moral framework embedded in explanations of why they should abandon their own traditions in favor of a more progressive, Western way of life.

Given that various interpretations of Darwin's theory have circulated through the discourses of the academic community for nearly 150 years—and frequently are now taken for granted—it is surprising that educational theorists have not turned natural selection into an explicit ideology that justifies why certain classes, cultures, technologies, and ideas succeed while others fail. It is a temptation that many other academics have been unable to resist. Educational psychologists' protracted but unsuccessful efforts to measure individual intelligence aside, educational theorists have largely relegated the Darwinian schema to the status of a commonsense understanding that the vitality of an experience involves "growth" (Dewey); that critical reflection will result in more progressive and thus socially evolved forms of praxis; that adopting more mechanistic ways of organizing classroom practices ensures that the best and most competitive system will win taxpayer approval and thus survive; and, in the latest expression of taken-for-granted Darwinian thinking, that a closer integration between schooling and the needs of the workplace will ensure that America will prevail in the global arena of economic and technological competition. Even for the Marxist educational theorists so prominent in the 1970s and 1980s, the evolutionary framework provided the temporal direction needed to identify certain groups as reactionary and thus in need of elimination.

On the whole, educational theorists concerned about the form of society being reinforced through the formal and informal curriculum have not yet succumbed to the *explicit* use of the theory of evolution. With scientists announcing almost daily the discovery of the genetic basis of illnesses, personality traits, and behaviors, however, it will become difficult to resist the gravitational pull of this new orthodoxy. The efforts of E. O. Wilson, Daniel Dennett, and Richard Alexander, among others, to explain the biological and thus evolutionary basis of cultural norms and practices will further undermine the resistance of theorists who want to bridge the gulf that still separates science from the more normative aspects of culture. The following discussion of the dangers of extending the theory of evolution to the cultural domain of education is intended to warn off educational theorists before they attempt to reconcile their liberal assumptions with the process of natural selection.

There is an elegant simplicity in Darwin's theory of natural selection that accounts for its growing status as *the* paradigm for understanding the dynamics of change and continuity in the natural world. Yet the scope of what it explains—the evolution of all natural phenomena, including humans and their artifacts and symbolic systems, over a period of four billion years—opens the door to interpretations that support ideologies of domination that can be extrapolated in ways that support the Western myth of progress. While Darwin did not foresee the development of computers and the accompanying cultural changes, his theory of evolutionary change can easily be expanded to fit this technology into the design process of nature. Even the sciences that are the basis of corporate efforts to genetically design plants and animals that fit the industrial model of production are being justified as representing a more evolved and better adapted way of knowing than the natural process they are replacing.

The following interpretations of the theory of evolution, as well as the scientific method on which it depends, indicate how easy it is to move from the supposedly nonpolitical domain of a scientific paradigm into the realm of ideology. In *The Demon-Haunted World: Science as a Candle in the Dark,* Carl Sagan answers his own question about which mode of knowing "is better geared to our long term survival" as follows:

> The reason science works so well is partly that built-in error-correcting machinery. There are no forbidden questions in science, no matters too sensitive or delicate to be probed, no sacred truths. That openness to new ideas, combined with the most rigorous, skeptical scrutiny of all ideas, sifts the wheat from the chaff. It makes no difference how smart, august, or beloved you are. You must prove your case in the face of determined, expert criticism. Diversity and debate are valued. Opinions are encouraged to contend— substantively and in depth. . . . We give our highest rewards to those who convincingly disprove established beliefs. (1997:34–35)

This mode of knowing has indeed made important contributions to our understanding of the natural world. It has also provided the basis for developing many useful technologies. But Sagan, like many other scientists, views science as the only legitimate approach to knowledge. And this is where the science and the theory of evolution, which is often wrongly equated by nonscientists with linear progress, leads to eco-justice abuses. Witness the observation that E. O. Wilson makes in *Consilience: The Unity of Knowledge:*

> Today the greatest divide within humanity is not between races, or religions, or even, as widely believed, between literate and illiterate. It is the chasm that separates scientific from prescientific cultures. Without the instruments and accumulated knowledge of the natural sciences—physics, chemistry, biology—humans are trapped in a cognitive prison. They are like intelligent fish born in a deep, shadowed pool. Wondering and restless, longing to reach out, they think about the world outside. They invent ingenious speculations and myths about the origin of the confining waters, of the sun and the sky and the stars above, and the meaning of their own existence. But they are wrong, always wrong, because the world is too remote from ordinary experience to be merely imagined. (1998b:45)

Wilson is a highly acclaimed scientist and leading spokesperson on the dangers of sliding into ecological collapse, and his pronouncements are taken seriously by the public—even as he claims that cultures that have not made Western science the capstone of their beliefs and values are "trapped in a cognitive prison." Ironically, while Wilson may view his effort to make the genocentric and evolutionary sciences the basis of all cultures, including the academic disciplines of Western-style universities, he is at the same time legitimizing the globalization process that is undermining cultures that have taken less ecologically destructive pathways to development. Wilson's assumption that the natural sciences are expressions of a more evolved way of thinking contains an implicit double bind; namely, the cultural assumptions that have guided the uses of Western science are largely responsible for the accelerated rate at which the environment is now being degraded—even as the sciences are used to study the scope and rate of that degradation.

What Wilson fails to recognize is that many cultures that have not assimilated the Western mindset have had to adapt their technologies and value systems to take account of the characteristics of their bioregions. Unlike one of the deepest assumptions underlying the modern/scientific mindset, these cultures do not take survival for granted. In effect, these prescientific cultures are repositories of intergenerational knowledge of how to balance the use of nature with communally centered lifestyles that do not have the side effect of turning the local environment into a toxic dump.

A third example of how evolution can be interpreted in a way that legitimizes an experimental approach to human-nature relationships can be seen in the conclusion that Kevin Kelly reaches in his book celebrating the spread of computer-mediated culture. In *Out of Control: The Rise of Neo-biological Civilization,* Kelly identifies the nine laws that operate in nature to produce, as he puts it, "something out of nothing." Kelly views this evolutionary process, which began with minerals and has now advanced to the manipulation of the genetic code, in ways that change the characteristics of plants and animals, as guiding the development of computer technology. Moral and political judgments about the direction of development are irrelevant, he insists: "We should not be surprised that life, having subjugated the bulk of inert matter on Earth, would go on to subjugate technology, and bring it also under its reign of constant evolution, perpetual novelty, and *an agenda out of our control.* Even without the control we must surrender, a neo-biological technology is far more rewarding than a world of clocks, gears, and predictable simplicity" (1994:472; italics added). The point that needs to be emphasized here is that, in Kelly's view, the design process of nature (i.e., evolution) will determine which technological and economic system—and thus which political system—will prevail. Put another way, the nonpolitical and amoral process of natural selection will determine what survives and what disappears—or, as understood by nineteenth-century Social Darwinists, the "survival of the fittest."

We can see in the above quotations more than an explanation of the nature of scientific thought and how natural selection accounts for the survival of organisms and technologies in terms of how well they are adapted to the forms of energy and competitiveness that constitute their environments. They also contain value judgments about which epistemology is to be used as the standard for judging other cultural ways of knowing. While Darwin understood the characteristics of culture in terms of the biological imperatives of heredity, adaptation through competitive interaction (which also involves cooperation), and reproduction, it is the more recent attempts to explain the biological basis of cultural norms and values that are the main concern here—which brings us to the writings of E. O. Wilson.

In *Sociobiology: The New Synthesis* (1975) and *On Human Nature* (1978), Wilson explains that a range of cultural practices, beliefs, and technologies are the result of evolution. This early effort to establish sociobiology as the centerpiece of the social sciences met with widespread criticism—in particular, that it was little more than an updated version of Social Darwinism. In spite of this criticism, Wilson has continued to refine the theory of "gene-culture coevolution." In *Consilience: The Unity of Knowledge,* he explains the causal connections between natural selection at the genetic level and the symbolic dimensions of culture:

> *Culture is created by the communal mind, and each mind in turn
> is the product of the genetically structured human brain. Genes and
> culture are therefore inseverably linked. But the linkage is flexible,
> to a degree still mostly unmeasured. The linkage is also tortuous:
> Genes prescribe epigenetic rules, which are the neural pathways and
> regularities in cognitive development by which the individual mind*

assembles itself. The mind grows from birth to death by absorbing
parts of the existing culture available to it, with selections guided
through epigenetic rules inherited by the individual brain.
(1998b:127; italics in original)

Wilson often introduces a qualification in order to avoid being interpreted as reducing all aspects of culture to their genetic determinants. But his efforts to provide a balanced interpretation are continually undermined by his inability to accept any explanation that does not have a biological basis. For example, in the *Atlantic Monthly* article titled "The Biological Basis of Morality" (1998a), he asserts that moral sentiments can best be understood through an "analysis of the underlying neural and endocrine responses." The genes that prescribe the chemical processes that we experience as moral norms are, in turn, the outcome of the evolutionary success of hundreds of previous generations that began on the grasslands of Africa. Simply put, what he refers to as the "religious instinct" is "hereditary, urged into existence through biases in mental development that are encoded in the genes" (1998a:65).

The word *meme*, first introduced into our vocabulary by Richard Dawkins in *The Selfish Gene* (1976), has a special place in Wilson's theory of gene-culture coevolution. Wilson suggests that the "unit of culture—now called meme—be [understood] as the node of semantic memory and its correlates in brain activity" (1998b:136). Presumably, this would mean that genetic differences account for differences in brain activity that lead, in turn, to the differences that exist between the Berber of North Africa, the Inuit of northern Canada, and the Apache of the American Southwest—as well as the differences among Jews, Protestants, Catholics, Buddhists, and Muslims.

Although Wilson continually refers to "gene-culture coevolution," the bottom line is that genes determine culture. Furthermore, the basic drive of the gene is to reproduce itself as part of the process of natural selection that prepares the organism (of which it is a constitutive part) to survive and reproduce itself in the ecological niche it occupies. This interpretation is identical to the "survival of the fittest" ideology of the late nineteenth century, except that Wilson shifts the locus of survival and reproductive success to the more basic level of how the genes go about the business of creating "survival machines." Following a disclaimer about suggesting that "a gene . . . prescribes culture," he gives the following explanation: "Thousands of genes prescribe the brain, the sensory system, and all the other physiological processes that interact with the physical and social environment to produce the holistic properties of mind and culture. *Through natural selection, the environment ultimately selects which genes will do the prescribing*" (Wilson 1998b:137; italics added). It is also important to understand the chemical environment in which the interplay of chance perturbations in the gene's environment and genetic fitness determines which evolutionary pathway organisms and cultures will follow. What the genes prescribe, and thus the Darwinian fitness of cultural patterns, is determined at a level over which human decision making has no direct influence. Indeed, what humans do, according to Wilson, has been determined by the process of natural selection. To restate a critical part of Dawkins's sociobiological argument, with which Wilson agrees: humans and other types of organisms are basically "survival machines [that] began as passive receptacles for the genes, providing little more than walls to protect them from the chemical warfare of their rivals and the ravages of accidental molecular bombardment" (1976:48).

To avoid misinterpretation, it is important to read Wilson's own explanation of what prescribes the direction of gene-culture coevolution—and thus what makes human decision making an illusion that, like religion, serves, according to this way of thinking, an adaptive purpose. In the chapter "Ariadne's Thread," Wilson writes:

> The machine the biologists have opened up is a creation of riveting beauty. At its heart are the nucleic acid codes, which in a typical vertebrate animal may comprise about 50,000 to 100,000 genes. Each gene is a string of 2,000 to 3,000 base pairs (genetic letters). Among the base pairs composing active genes, each triplet (set of three) translates into an amino acid. The final molecular products of the genes, as transcribed outward through the cell by scores of perfectly orchestrated chemical reactions, are sequences of amino acids folded into giant protein molecules. There are about 100,000 kinds of protein in a vertebrate animal. Where the nucleic acids are the codes, the proteins are the substance of life, making up half the animal's dry weight. They give form to the body, hold it together by collagen sinews, move it by muscle, catalyze all its animating chemical reactions, transport oxygen to all its parts, arm the immune system, and carry the signals by which the brain scans the environment and mediates behavior. (1998b:91)

It is important not to allow the lucidity of Wilson's explanation, and his personal sense of awe, to obscure the main point here: namely, that these chemical processes signal "how the brain scans the environment and mediates behavior." That is, the phrase "gene-culture coevolution" should not be interpreted to mean that there are other ways of accounting for the development of cultural semiotic systems and technologies than the process of natural selection.

It would be wrong to conclude that Wilson is a lone Prometheus attempting to bring the sacred narrative of evolution to enlighten a world in darkness. The number of books written by Western academics arguing that cultures evolve through the process of natural selection is both astonishing and alarming—if one considers the ideological implications of this literature. The following titles suggest the range of academic disciplines now being influenced by conceptual reformulations that are in line with Wilson's arguments: Ellen Dissanayake, *Homo Aestheticus: Where Art Comes from and Why* (1992); Merlin Donald, *Origins of the Modern Mind: Three Stages in the Evolution of Culture and Cognition* (1991); Ray Kurzweil, *The Age of Spiritual Machines: When Computers Exceed Human Intelligence* (1999); Steven Pinker, *The Language Instinct: How the Mind Creates Language* (1995); Robert Storey, *Mimesis and the Human Animal: On the Biogenetic Foundations of Literary Representation* (1996); Frans B. M. de Waal, *Good Natured: The Origins of Right and Wrong in Humans and Other Animals* (1996); and Robert Wright, *The Moral Animal: Evolutionary Psychology and Everyday Life* (1994).

At the risk of appearing to go against Nature's design processes, I would like to summarize the eco-justice issues raised by the increasingly widespread adoption of the evolution metanarrative. I hope that the list below will influence educational reformers to avoid the cultural extrapolations that scientists and other academics seem so eager to make. It is also my hope that Nature has not already earmarked educational theorists for extinction—though I am aware that people in the computer industry, having already reached this conclusion, are working to replace them (as well as other academics) with computers.

While not all biologists share Wilson's genocentric interpretation of evolution, many consider it the most advanced interpretation of Darwin's basic explanation of how the survival of species is the outcome of the forces of inheritance, random variation, and natural selection. Given the media spotlight on genocentric research and technologies, these basic Darwinian metaphors are likely to be accepted as having the supreme authority that Sagan wants to accord to the scientific method of thinking. In addition to the authority of science, which most university graduates have learned to accept without questioning, economic, political, and technological forces behind the process of globalization continue to be justified through the use of a language that restates the basic processes of natural selection. Extinction of organisms and cultures, as the evolution narrative holds, has nothing to do with the moral qualities or mythopoetic narratives that frame relationships within communities and between humans and the environment. While Wilson and others may view human communities as functionally adapted for survival, the displacement of some cultures by others that are both more technologically efficient and less burdened by misguided concerns with the plight of low achievers can easily be justified on the ground that dominance, in whatever form it takes, is Nature's way of rewarding the better adapted and thus the fittest.

The following list of "better-adapted" technologies, moral norms, economic systems, and cultural epistemology is identical with the list of eco-justice issues that need to be addressed at all levels of the educational process:

1. Globalization of Western technology that requires greater dependence on consumerism while at the same time reducing the opportunity for meaningful work.

2. Globalization of the Western model of development that leads to loss of cultural diversity—including the disappearance of languages that encode intergenerational knowledge of local ecosystems.

3. Globalization of Western technology that leads to the loss of skills and systems of mutual support required by relatively self-reliant communities.

4. Globalized use of genetically engineered plants that displace indigenous agricultural knowledge and reduce the ability of naturally evolved species to reproduce themselves while at the same time integrating the production of food into the industrial

model that requires increasing amounts of capital and use of environmentally destructive chemicals.

5. Globalization of digital technologies, industrial models of production, and capitalism that forces less adapted cultures to turn their environments into exportable products and to accept the toxic wastes of the more genetically fit Western cultures.

6. Globalization that increases the economic wealth of the North while further impoverishing the South.

7. Globalization of the modern mindset based on the premise that the individual is the basic social unit, that consumerism is the primary source of happiness and success, and that the extinction of intergenerational responsibility is an inevitable aspect of social evolution.

This list of eco-justice issues has been framed in terms of the current ideology promoting globalization and a world monoculture. Each issue has equally complex ramifications for the local level, where cultural, regional, urban/rural, and environmental differences come into play. Zoning laws that result in the poor being exposed to more toxic chemicals, corporations that promote closer integration of education with the workplace, and classroom teachers who encourage "constructivist" learning that makes students more vulnerable to media manipulation and thus to consumerism can all be interpreted in terms of the Darwinian theory that explains why the "fittest" prevail and the less fit become extinct. Indeed, the interplay of inheritance, random selection, and survival of the better adapted can easily be understood as supporting the theories of Prigogine and Whitehead.

One can only hope that educational theorists' long-term concerns about social equity and the plight of groups that have been impoverished by the latest manifestations of the Industrial Revolution will enable them to recognize that those who extrapolate the cultural implications of Darwin's updated theory are simply restating the basic tenets of Social Darwinism. One must further hope that educational theorists will at last recognize the historical connections between the different genres of educational liberalism and the form of individualism required by the Industrial Revolution. Articulating the nature of a pedagogy that challenges the idea of better-adapted cultural patterns (memes), and thus addresses the eco-justice issues that emerge from the experiences of subjugated cultural groups, will be even more difficult—particularly as most education professors have been socialized to think in a language that encodes the deep cultural assumptions that have guided the development of the high-status culture now being touted as the universal model of development. Frequent reports on the rapid degradation of various ecosystems, as well as reports of resistance to the biological and digital technologies that are changing community patterns of interdependence into new forms of dependence on experimental forms of knowledge, will serve as constant reminders that these assumptions cannot be taken for granted as ensuring our collective survival.

3 Educational Computing

Jacques Ellul, the French philosopher of technology, observed that once a technology has been integrated into a culture's daily routines it is impossible to reverse directions by going back to an earlier form. This is undoubtedly the case with computer technology. It mediates and governs nearly every aspect of modern life—from scientific inquiry, medical practice, and operations of government and business to education and personal entertainment. It is difficult to imagine how major airports could operate without computers or how scientists could track major changes in natural systems without the computer's ability to measure and model the changes. But this dependence on computers should not be taken to mean that the future transformations of the world's cultures envisioned by computer scientists and ideologues are inevitable—as some are now claiming.

Computers are not a culturally neutral technology; anyone who has reflected on the forms of knowledge and relationships that cannot be accommodated by computers should be keenly aware of this. Yet this seemingly obvious fact has been overlooked for a number of reasons that can be traced to the widespread habit of equating technological innovation with social progress, and to the belief that it is the user rather than the technology that determines its impact. And just as both critics and devotees seem oblivious to the culture-transforming characteristics of computers, the eco-justice issues associated with the spread of computer-based technologies and social relationships are also being ignored. This is especially the case among educators who are overcoming their earlier reluctance to substitute computer-mediated learning for the long-standing tradition of face-to-face interaction.

The ubiquity of computers in daily life now needs to be matched by an equally widespread public discussion of the cultural gains and losses associated with the mediating characteristics of computers. Specifically, there is a need to consider eco-justice issues that range from the morality of globalizing a hyperdependent consumer- and technology-oriented culture to more community-centered issues related to the loss of knowledge and commitment to place, participation, and intergenerational renewal. The role of computers in determining which cultural groups gain and lose economically is also an exceedingly complex issue. It is unlikely that the media can be relied on to foster a discussion of these issues because publishers and broadcasters are becoming increasingly dependent on advertising revenues. Other institutions and social groups, such as churches and environmentalist organizations, have agendas that reflect the limitations of their own educational experience, and thus are not likely to provide the proper forum. How many people associated with a religious or environmental group, for example, can identify how the culture-mediating characteristics of computers contribute to the moral and environmental problems they are attempting to address? Businesses, large and small, and local and national service organizations are even less likely venues for a sustained public discussion that would represent the first step toward democratizing technology.

Since I wrote *Cultural Literacy for Freedom* in 1974 I have been arguing that public school and university classrooms are virtually the only places where students can examine cultural and environmental issues free of the penalties that would be encountered in the workplace or other social settings. Over the years I have become increasingly aware of the double bind inherent in this argument—a double bind that also explains why my arguments have been largely ignored. When I shifted my attention from how education contributes to carrying forward the patterns of thinking that are exacerbating the ecological crisis to the teachers and professors who are being urged to recognize their responsibilities in this area, the double bind became obvious. Even though public school teachers and university professors are generally not restricted by outside forces from engaging students in an examination of the deep cultural assumptions on which their views of technology and natural systems are based, their own lack of education regarding these fundamental relationships and dependencies prevents them from doing so. The language within which most educators first learned to think and communicate encoded the metaphorical constructions of an earlier cultural period when progress was taken to be synonymous with controlling and exploiting the endless resources of nature. And they, in turn, reproduce the same deep cultural schemata in their classrooms and still view language as a conduit in a sender-receiver process of communication—as a neutral technology. The double bind thus continues to exist in most classrooms: the modern way of thinking that arose at the time of the Industrial Revolution is reinforced in students who will have to cope with radically degraded ecosystems, a burgeoning world population that is adopting the material expectations of the West, and a scientific-corporate alliance that is focused on the development of computer technology.

In spite of this double bind, the classroom remains the most viable site for providing the knowledge necessary for an informed public discussion of the eco-justice issues raised by the dominant cultural approach to technology. Others will argue that the Internet is now the main arena of public debate and source of knowledge. However, this argument does not take into account the rapid commercialization of the Internet or the fact that the marginalized cultural groups most adversely affected by modern technology and values are unlikely to be actively involved in chat rooms and electronic interest groups. In effect, the economic resources required for participating in the Internet combined with some cultural groups' reluctance to communicate via decontextualized printed words on a computer screen work against the equal representation of the cultural groups that most need to be part of the public effort to democratize technology.

If the challenge in 1974 was to increase awareness of the connection between what was being taught in our classrooms and the ecological crisis, the challenge today is to foster an awareness that the background knowledge essential for communicative competence in addressing today's most pressing issues must be learned in the classroom. The issues range from biotechnology, the commercialization of electronic media, and the creation of a global financial system that can destabilize a country's economic system overnight to the increasing dependence on educational software as the primary means of cultural renewal. Getting public school teachers and university professors to recognize the importance of examining how technology is interwoven into nearly every aspect of modern culture and how Western technologies undermine what remains of the self-sufficiency of non-Western cultures remains a particularly daunting challenge. One starting point for fostering a sense of responsibility for reforming the curriculum is to consider the utopian vision that computer scientists and ideologues are working toward.

Replacing Humans with Machines

A common element in the thinking of such computer visionaries as Hans Moravec, Gregory Stock, and Ray Kurzweil is the belief that computers eventually will be able to perform like humans—including being able to produce literature, communicate human-like emotions, and replicate the characteristics of consciousness. For them, the increasing dominance of computers in the process of Darwinian evolution makes the realization of these possibilities only a matter of time. While the claims of Sherry Turkle and Nicholas Negroponte that cyberspace expands individual experience in radically new ways are difficult enough to substantiate, the prediction that computers will displace humans in the evolutionary process has even more profound implications. My concern is not that the linear view of progress they have superimposed on the process of natural selection makes their predication more mythically based than grounded in an understanding of the design process that operates in nature. Far more alarming is the fact that computer scientists, driven by good intentions and the quest to pursue knowledge and develop technologies that push back the frontiers of the unknown, are extending the use of computers in ways that are increasingly displacing human activity—even to providing substitutes for human organs and physical capabilities. Many of these developments represent genuine contributions to improving the quality of life for individuals. But this drive to augment and, increasingly, to replace human functions with machines— the ubiquitous automated personality that announces the many options available when we make a phone inquiry comes to mind here—is not accompanied by a public discussion of how machines degrade the quality of human relationships.

Researchers working in biotechnology have made the cloning of human beings a possibility that will certainly be exploited by some scientist more interested in establishing a place in history than in waiting for the moral questions involved to be fully explored and settled. And computer visionaries such as Ray Kurzweil are praising the efforts of scientists working on the development of a quantum computer that has equally unexamined implications. According to Kurzweil, "a 40-qu-bit quantum computer will be able to evaluate a trillion possible solutions simultaneously" (1999:113). Such efforts to develop technologies that far exceed the capacity of the human brain give a false degree of credibility to the even more extreme claim that humans, as Hans Moravec puts it in *Mind Children: The Future of Robot and Human Intelligence* (1988), are entering a "postbiological world dominated by self-improving machines" (5).

Moravec further predicts that at the next stage in the evolutionary process the content of the human brain will be downloaded into computers that have already evolved along the pathway of designing even more advanced forms of machine intelligence. Gregory Stock, who holds a Ph.D. in biophysics from Johns Hopkins University, interprets this evolution as displacing vernacular cultures with a global superorganism that he calls "Metaman." He describes the transition from the diverse cultural ways of knowing that now exist to the global mind (Metaman) in the following way: "Continually sensing, transferring, and manipulating information, Metaman does more than just shuffle and store data. Metaman interprets and processes. In essence, Metaman actually 'thinks' by using a 'brain' that literally is all around us. And that brain contains within it the functional equivalent of a global 'memory' housing all of humanity's accumulated knowledge. Examining the evolution of this global memory reveals its nature and future" (1993:84–85). Like Turkle, Stock's vision of the global superorganism retains the core features of our hyperconsumer culture. That he views the global spread of Metaman as a part of the natural process whereby less evolved cultures (as he perceives them) are displaced by better adapted ones highlights again the failure of computer proponents to understand the moral and ecological implications of their techno-utopian vision.

Ray Kurzweil's most recent book, *The Age of Spiritual Machines: When Computers Exceed Human Intelligence* (1999), is even more remarkable—and disturbing. Kurzweil, the recipient of nine honorary doctorates and the intelligence behind four computer start-up companies, brings a level of applied theoretical knowledge to his vision of a techno-utopia that has long been the staple of science fiction writers. Unfortunately, his vast knowledge of cutting-edge developments in computer technology is not matched by an awareness of its possible consequences for the Earth and its inhabitants. Kurzweil is typical of an elite group of computer scientists and engineers who are so driven by the assumption that their efforts are the latest expression of the evolutionary process that they see no need to inform themselves about the cultural and environmental losses that will result from their work. He and other computer-based visionaries interpret advances in computer technology as making only a positive contribution to the quality of life. They ignore the ways computers degrade community life because these cannot be measured objectively and are difficult to assess in terms of market value.

The following predictions by Kurzweil of the future of humanity are especially noteworthy for their lack of wisdom (and even common sense).

On downloading the human mind into a computer:

Objectively, when we scan someone's brain and reinstantiate their personal mind file into a suitable computing medium, the newly emergent "person" will appear to other observers to have very much the same personality, history, and memory as the person originally scanned. Interacting with the newly instantiated person will feel like interacting with the original person. The new person will claim to be that same old person and will have a memory of having been that person, having grown up in Brooklyn, having walked into a scanner here, and woken up in the machine there. He'll say, "Hey, this technology really works." (1999:125)

On the end of mortality:

Actually there won't be mortality by the end of the twenty-first century. Not in the sense that we have known it. Not if you take advantage of the twenty-first century's brain-porting technology. Up until now, our mortality was tied to the longevity of our *hardware*. When the hardware crashed, that was it. For many of our forebears, the hardware gradually deteriorated before it disintegrated. . . . As we cross the divide to instantiate ourselves in our computational technology, our identity will be based on our evolving mind file. . . . Our immortality will be a matter of being sufficiently careful to make frequent backups. If we're careless about this, we'll have to load an old backup copy and be doomed to repeat our recent past. (128–129)

On virtual houses of worship for spiritual machines:

Neuroscientists from the University of California at San Diego have found what they call the God module, a tiny locus of nerve cells in the frontal lobe that appears to be activated during religious experiences. . . . When we can determine the neurological correlates of the variety of spiritual experiences that our species is capable of, we are likely to be able to enhance these experiences in the same way that we will enhance other human experiences. With the next stage of evolution creating a new generation of humans that will be trillions of times more capable and complex than humans today, our ability for spiritual experience and insight is also likely to gain in power and depth. . . . Twenty-first century machines—based on the design of human thinking—will do as their human progenitors have done—going to real and virtual houses of worship, meditating, praying, and transcending—to connect with their spiritual dimension. (152–153)

What motivates Kurzweil and other techno-utopian thinkers who envision the creation of nonbiological entities that can pass themselves off as humans deserves special analysis that goes beyond the main concerns of this chapter. However, several observations will help connect the mythic thinking of Kurzweil with the only slightly less mythic thinking of the proponents of a digitized educational process.

The messianic spirit that once drove the expansion of Christianity has now become secularized and has been taken over by scientists. That is, the quest now is to push technological innovation beyond the present horizon of possibility; for example, Kurzweil's proposal to install human thoughts and emotions in a new computational medium that will have the power of a "trillion human brains by the year 2060." The messianic drive to surpass previous levels of technological development that is evident in Kurzweil's microchip version of the new Jerusalem must also be understood as being motivated by an industry that now generates more than $1.755 trillion a year in income—more than the amount earned by four-fifths of the U.S. population.

The desire to achieve professional acclaim is part of the mix of motivations that drive the Kurzweils of the computer industry. But perhaps even more important is the narrowness of their university education, which has left them unable to recognize that the vast majority of the world's population does not share their priorities or dreams. In effect, their specialized education prevents them from recognizing the basic questions that need to be asked: Why do we need machines that will be indistinguishable from humans? Will the environment be able to survive the ecological footprint of Metaman? Shouldn't our resources be used to deepen our moral understanding of the relationships that characterize the layered and interdependent ecologies that connect cultures to the natural world? Will the ability to process billions of "bits" of information simultaneously help people with different cultural ways of knowing learn to respect each other's approaches to community?

The merging of the evolution metanarrative with the Western myth of linear progress also dominates the thinking of educators, corporate spokespersons, and politicians who think that the widest possible classroom use of computers will guarantee America's dominance in the global economy. They view the vast expenditure required to put computers in classrooms, connect public schools and universities to the Internet, train teachers how to integrate computers into the curriculum, and purchase the educational soft-ware and upgrades in equipment as the start of an education revolution. The ultimate goal of this revolution is to replace the face-to-face relationships in traditional classrooms with virtual learning technologies that, supposedly, will be more cost-effective and more directly controllable by public school and university administrators.

Typical of the current rush to embrace computers as the panacea for the nation's economic and educational shortcomings is the *Report to the President on the Use of Technology to Strengthen K–12 Education in the United States* written by the President's Committee of Advisors on Science and Technology. The report recommends that total expenditure on computer-mediated learning in grades K–12 be increased from the current level of 1.3 percent of education budgets to at least 5 percent—which would come to more than $13 billion annually. The report also states that "student initiated" learning could best be facilitated if based on constructivist learning principles (although the report acknowledges these as still unproven).

There is a corresponding rush on the part of the nation's universities to exploit the market for degrees earned in cyberspace. Administrative pressure on professors to put their courses online and to interact with students in chat rooms is also increasing. In effect, university administrators view cyberspace as a cash cow. The promise of software able to evaluate written examinations is being interpreted as yet another reason for substituting programmable machines for tenured professors. The pressure exerted by corporations on university administrators to substitute computers for professors is motivated by their perception that higher education represents a multi-billion-dollar market waiting to be exploited. Given the extent to which public schools and universities already promote values that support a consumer-oriented culture, it is not surprising that this effort to integrate education into the latest expression of industrial commodification is meeting with only token resistance. Students taking online classes find them mechanical and devoid of intellectual stimulation. Yet they also find them personally convenient and a source of socialization to the workplace they are about to enter. Although the faculty at several American universities and at York University in Canada openly resisted efforts to dictate the use of computers as part of the instructional process, most faculties have complied and incorporated computers when it seemed appropriate to the content of their courses. Overall, faculties seem indifferent to the structural and economic consequences of the trend now sweeping through universities. Substantive criticism has been largely limited to the writings of David Noble, Langdon Winner, and Theodore Roszak. The long-standing bias within universities against studying technology as a cultural phenomenon, and thus as an essential part of a liberal education, accounts in part for the ambivalence. The few expressions of concern have largely been limited to issues relating to job security and the loss of face-to-face contact with students. But these potential sources of resistance have been mitigated by the usefulness of computers in conducting research and in communicating with colleagues in different parts of the world. Most faculties judge the advantages in these areas more important than educational losses—with the latter being particularly difficult to articulate.

Even professors who think within an intellectual tradition that has long been critical of capitalism seem unable to recognize how the culture-mediating characteristics of computers reinforce the key features of the Industrial Revolution. For example, in "Critical Pedagogy and Cyberspace," Colin Lankshear, Michael Peters, and Michele Knobel write that "critical pedagogy is most definitely a viable educational enterprise within cyberspace. Indeed, many of its functional concepts and principles are made more explicit and more relevant within the educational expanses of cyberspace" (1996:149). They further claim that "in cyberspace . . . democracy is realized implicitly and as an underlying principle" (163) and that the forms of authority that negate the possibility of educational empowerment are absent from cyberspace. The advantages of cyberspace they cite include its vast store of information, the individual experience of deciding which borders to cross, the ability to exchange ideas without the inhibiting influence of status differences, the opportunity to experiment with one's personal identity, and the experience of contingent cultural norms and practices. "Just as critical pedagogy in cyberspace provides possibilities for transforming classroom practice along more democratic lines," they say, "so the insights, information, and exposure to differences and experiences of solidarity gleaned from encounters in cyberspace enhance the prospects of individual and collective action aimed at transforming social practices and relations outside the classroom" (185). As I pointed out earlier, many liberal and left-oriented educational theorists take for granted the deep cultural assumptions that continue to provide conceptual direction and moral legitimacy to the Industrial Revolution. The digital phase of this continuing revolution is thus seen as simply the latest expression of the need for constant change, greater individual empowerment, and the globalization of the antitradition traditions that many Western theorists mistakenly view as the source of democracy and social justice.

Just as there is a double bind in locating the justifications for an ecologically sustainable future in the traditions of Western liberalism, there is also a double bind in criticizing technology (specifically, computers) from a liberal perspective. Both the ideals found in the different genres of liberalism and the forces of hyper-commodification unleashed by the Industrial Revolution require the type of individualism that is the antithesis of the community and place-centered individualism described in the quotation taken from Sale's *Rebels against the Future* (see the Introduction). By way of contrast, a cultural/bio-conservative conceptual and moral framework leads to the following criticisms of computer-mediated learning. Proponents of educational computing appear to have transferred the conventional way of thinking of language as a conduit through which ideas are communicated from one person to another to how they think about computers. The widely held assumption about the neutral nature of technology has further made it appear unnecessary to ask about the mediating characteristics of computers—a question that goes much deeper than asking about the cultural assumptions encoded in the conceptual and moral content of educational software. When computers are understood to be merely a conduit in a sender-receiver process of communication, the issue of cultural mediation will not come up. A primary characteristic of computers that is often overlooked is that they are a language-processing technology. And contrary to popular belief, language is not a neutral conduit. This can be seen in the way the root metaphors of a cultural group frame the process of analogical thinking and are encoded in the iconic metaphors shaped by earlier processes of analogical thinking. The culturally specific assumptions embedded in the language that appears on the computer screen (anthropocentrism, mechanism, linear progress, etc.) are evident in educational software such as *SimCity* and *SimEarth*. The counterargument might be made that the cultural non-neutrality of language should not be considered as evidence that computers privilege certain forms of knowledge and communication, and thus some cultural groups over others. The weakness of this argument is obvious when we take into account the fact that computers can process and model thought only in a decontextualized language system—which is profoundly different from face-to-face communication (which also encodes the layers of metaphorical constructions of a specific cultural group). Face-to-face communication is always contextualized and is not a sender-receiver process of communication. That is, it involves personal memories, patterns of metacommunication, and individualized interpretation of cultural patterns formed over generations of collective experience.

When the full range of evidence is considered, it becomes obvious that the thought patterns reinforced by the mediating characteristics of computers are identical with the high-status, decontextualized ways of thinking that underlie the Industrial Revolution. It also becomes easier to recognize that the patterns of communication and forms of knowledge that cannot be communicated through a computer are what knit together ecologically coherent communities. To computer experts who assume that all aspects of culture can be digitized and thus processed through a computer, these criticisms may seem utter nonsense. But that is because they have not asked about the forms of knowledge and communication excluded by the culture-mediating characteristics of computers. The most plausible explanation of why this question has not been asked can be traced back to the distinction between high- and low-status forms of knowledge promoted in universities. The latter, which includes the noncommodified, face-to-face, intergenerational, embodied, convivial, place-specific, and mutual support experiences of everyday life, takes on significance only when some dimension of it can be turned into a niche market for a new technology. The effort to sell computers to grandparents so they can e-mail their children and grandchildren is a good example.

As I have discussed elsewhere the mediating characteristics of computers (Bowers 1988, 1995, 1997, 2000), I will merely summarize them here and then go on to address the question of how these mediating characteristics relate to an eco-justice pedagogy. The connection between the cultural mindset reinforced by computers and eco-justice issues needs to be understood if we are to avoid the mistake of assuming that computer literacy is part of the solution to inequities in class, race, and gender.

The following forms of cultural mediation are integral characteristics of computers that will be further masked as the technology shifts toward voice commands and toward incorporating emotional and olfactory dimensions of experience (which will still, of course, be culturally specific).

Computers can process only explicit and decontextualized thoughts, forms of expression, and cultural patterns. Cultural patterns that are taken for granted cannot be digitized, and thus cannot be communicated through a computer. When the patterns are made explicit and digitized, they are taken out of the context of shared meanings and tacit understandings of traditional relationships and moral norms—which means they become abstract and fundamentally changed. The key issue here is that tacit cultural patterns and understandings, including the patterns of metacommunication, encode different cultural ways of knowing and historical experiences.

In *Hombres y Machos: Masculinity and Latino Culture,* Alfredo Mirande gives the example of the word *pelado,* which defies simple translation. While it literally means "plucked," "naked," or "stripped" and connotes a lowly person, a nobody, Mirande notes that it encodes the historical memory of the rape and devastation of the land and its people by the Spanish conquistadors. It also denotes both positive and negative qualities—depending on the context in which it is used (1997:37–39). The context, perspective, layers of class and gendered memory, and intent behind the use of the word are eliminated by the mediating characteristics of the computer. In effect, the computer transforms the deeply contextual and cultural into what can be abstractly represented on the screen. The computer, in other words, perpetuates the Western tradition of discrimination against oral traditions. Giving computers the ability to communicate in scripted voices will not fundamentally alter the fact that *context* and *tacit* cultural understandings cannot be programmed.

Computers amplify a way of thinking that assumes that data is the basis of thought and that language (words, grammatical patterns) is a neutral technology that allows ideas, information, and data to be communicated to others. It is impossible for computers to be programmed in such a way that the history and culturally specific nature of the metaphorical language appearing on the screen can be made explicit. Nor can the computer be programmed to interact with the interpretation that the individual brings to the metaphorical language appearing on the screen. That is, computers reinforce the representational function of language. This view of language, which is essential to sustaining the cultural myth of objective knowledge, involves the assumption that words stand for and thus represent real entities and have universal meanings. At the same time, computers obscure the metaphorical nature of language— that is, the fact that language encodes the root metaphors and earlier processes of a cultural group's analogical thinking. The elites of other cultures often communicate in ways that are easily understood by Western thinkers, reinforcing the myth of words having universal meanings, because they have been largely educated in Western universities and think within the epistemic patterns of the English language.

The conduit view of language, the privileging of print-based thought and communication, and the decontextualized nature of the words and visual models appearing on the screen serve to reinforce the Western assumption that the individual is an autonomous social being. These mediating characteristics strengthen the Western cultural emphasis on individualized perspective, interpretation, and choice as being hallmarks of our autonomous individuality. The experience of self as integral to a dynamic web of reciprocal relationships, or as having an identity that includes the extended family (and even a cultural group), cannot be communicated through a computer. Regardless of whether printed words appear on the screen or the interaction is with a scripted voice that does not have a regional accent, the computer reinforces the Western view of the individual.

Computer-mediated thought and communication reinforce the modern, individual-centered experience of temporality: that is, how the past, present, and future are experienced. Like earlier print-based technology, computers reinforce the Western cultural experience of a spectator relationship to the past and future. They foster the sense that the present moment in time provides the vantage point for looking back into the past or forward into the future and deciding whether either should be taken into account in terms of the immediate moment of decision making. To put this another way, the relevance of past and future are contingent on the emotive and rational judgment of the individual. This is radically different from the experience of temporality in cultures in which past and future are experienced as part of the living present. The traditional practice of some indigenous cultures in North America of framing decisions in terms of the well-being of the seventh unborn generation contrasts sharply with the experience of temporality reinforced by computers.

While modern individuals are engaged in computer-mediated activities they are reenacting simultaneously a wide range of traditions that are not recognized as traditions because of their taken-for-granted status. And because these traditions (spellings, use of paragraphs, layout of the keyboard, use of root metaphors, and so forth) have become integral to their natural attitude toward everyday life, they are present sources of empowerment. In effect, computers foster what can only be called an illusory sense of time, diverting awareness from the many viable traditions that are being undermined by computer technology. For example, the traditional norms governing the distinction between our private and public lives have been disappearing with each "advance" in the use of computers. The way computers amplify the modern bias that traditions are restrictive and outmoded while at the same time reinforcing an awareness of time that is subjectively determined ensures that the value of traditions will not be recognized until after they have been lost. At that point they cannot be recovered, but this is not a fact that worries the citizen of cyberspace. Members of cultural groups that still experience traditions and the future as sources of authority and responsibility in making decisions find that using the computer can be a conflicted experience—especially if they still value the traditions that constitute their interculturalist lifestyle and self-identity.

The fact that they must be purchased and that there are other costs connected with their use means that computers commodify the most basic activities and relationships: thought and communication. Even if computers were made freely available to everybody, they still would be part of the industrial culture—and they would still operate as a colonizing technology. The current rush to turn cyberspace into an electronic shopping mall and thus to further undermine the economic viability of the small businesses that constitute the heart of towns and cities indicates how computers make consumerism an ever more ubiquitous aspect of people's lives. Traditional shopping in the town center provides for social interaction that knits the community together. Shopping on the Internet, while seemingly more convenient, further reduces the need to interact with other people and eliminates the possibility that a wide range of issues and events might become part of the conversation. It also eliminates the small producer and other workers who are necessary for the economic life of the community. The Internet, in effect, further strengthens the trend toward centralization of production and distribution of goods and services in ways that maximize the economy of scale for corporations. At the same time, the Internet reduces the accountability and community-building relationships characteristic of small-scale local producers.

Eco-Justice Issues Associated with Computers

Although computers are represented as a watershed technology that is ushering in a new and radically different era, a more accurate way to understand their effects on cultures can be gained by putting their culture-amplifying characteristics into historical perspective. Specifically, these characteristics—print-based decontextualized thought, the autonomous individual who relies on data as the source of ideas, an individual-centered view of time that makes traditions and the future contingent on subjective mood and rational self-interest, a view of language that reinforces the assumption that intelligence is an individual attribute rather than the individualizing of a shared cultural episteme—need to be examined in terms of their antecedents. The similarities between Kirkpatrick Sale's description of the type of individual required for the success of the early phase of the Industrial Revolution and the form of individualism reinforced by computers come immediately to mind here. And just as there was then a conflict followed by an assimilation that had disastrous consequences for the environment, there continues to be a conflict between the digital phase of the Industrial Revolution and cultural groups who are attempting to resist the pressures of Western modernism. Indeed, the failed efforts of the Luddites are a metaphor for today's process of globalization.

Although Negroponte claims that "computing is not about computers any more. It is about living" (1995:6), there are a number of cultural activities that cannot be digitized and communicated through a computer. And the list of what cannot be digitized is remarkably similar to a list of the characteristics of cultural groups that have developed relatively self-reliant communities. These characteristics include:

> face-to-face activities that represent the range of noncommodified activities and relationships that constitute the life of the community;

> the forms of knowledge and relationships essential to learning the norms governing moral reciprocity;

> narratives of how the ecologies of family and community are anchored in the ecology of place;

> the process of mentoring that combines the development of character with the development of individual talents;

> ceremonies that renew the community's symbolic and moral foundations;

patterns of metacommunication that strengthen relationships and facilitate communication;

and participation in the intergenerational life of the community in ways that discard outmoded traditions and create new

ones that take into account the well-being of future generations. The wide variation in how these participatory and embodied patterns of community are expressed by different cultural groups cannot be communicated through a computer. They can be digitized in a documentary format. Others can learn from them and view them as a source of entertainment. But regardless of how many people view the documentary as a contribution to an educational process, it is part of the process of commodification that reinforces the cultural patterns associated with the autonomous individual who enters the experience as a spectator. In effect, abstract representations of other cultural practices and beliefs such as those found in *National Geographic* or on public television are an aspect of consumer society.

In identifying the patterns of community life that are transformed into an abstract, decontextualized representation when communicated through a computer, I am not suggesting that all community patterns—mentoring, narrativizing, ceremonies, and so forth—are morally equal and environmentally viable. The recent "ethnic cleansing" in the Balkans and similar events in other parts of the world suggest that this is not the case. Nor am I suggesting that all forms of electronic communities reinforce a particular form of individualism and cultural way of knowing. The point is more fundamental—namely, that the very nature of computers leads to certain cultural patterns being reinforced over others. Ideally, this should lead, in turn, to asking how the cultural patterns reinforced, as well as those marginalized or directly undermined, affect the environment and the quality of community life.

The globalization of computer technology is accelerating the spread of the industrial model of development, and the expansion of consumer markets and the adaptation of agriculture and education practices to fit this model of development are becoming the highest priority of national governments. In addition, the continuing centralization of political and economic power in the interlocking system of international corporations is increasingly dependent on the computer's ability to process vast amounts of data and provide near-instantaneous communication on a global scale. Corporations promoting the World Trade Organization, the North American Free Trade Agreement, and the General Agreement on Tariffs and Trade, as well as the recently failed effort to establish a Multinational Agreement on Investment, are trying to create a monoculture of dependency. If they succeed, they will control the manufacture of products ranging from cars to pharmaceuticals, standardized consumer buying habits, biotechnology-dependent agriculture, and entertainment. The extension of international patents to genetically altered microorganisms, plants, and animals represents yet another way in which local cultures are being integrated into a money economy—and thus being led further along the road to impoverishment. Multinational corporations are working to integrate the youth of different cultures into the global market by connecting brand-name sports and entertainment products with high fashion. They are also involved in the production of curricula for use in schools and in targeting youth culture as a distinct multibillion-consumer market.

The culture-amplifying characteristics of computers raise a wide range of eco-justice issues that have direct implications for what is learned in public school and university classrooms. Unfortunately, those who want to make students completely dependent on computers are not considering these implications. Nor are they being considered by reformers who view computer literacy as a way of alleviating the material conditions of poverty. Every cultural group needs to have access to the technologies that are the basis of today's employment and communication. But they also need to understand that there are tradeoffs and that the loss of face-to-face traditions that accompanies the transition to the decontextualized realm of cyberspace may lead to more important forms of impoverishment. There is little likelihood that the computer industry, in constant search of profits, can be counted on to help the public achieve a more balanced understanding of the appropriate and inappropriate uses of computers. In fact, their concern with economic growth combined with a desire to limit education to the technical knowledge necessary to design new computer-related technologies make the spokespersons for the industry a powerful source of miseducation. Witness such books as Bill Gates's *The Road Ahead,* Nicholas Negroponte's *Being Digital,* Esther Dyson's *Release 2.0: A Design for Living in the Digital Age,* and Ray Kurzweil's *The Age of Spiritual Machines: When Computers Exceed Human Intelligence.*

The differences between modern and traditional technologies and the culture-mediating characteristics of computers are critical elements of an eco-justice pedagogy. Democratizing decisions about the cultural and ecological gains and losses associated with computers and other technologies such as biotechnology must start in an educational setting. As the dominant culture does not have a tradition of elders reminding us of the relationships and values essential to morally coherent communities, and because few parents possess the background knowledge or personal inclination, the classroom remains the only viable site for this process to begin. The double bind implicit in suggesting that public school teachers and university professors should take on a task that represents an area of deficiency in their own educational background is addressed in the next two chapters.

4 Elements of an Eco-Justice Curriculum

The experts responsible for creating the technologies that are now undermining cultural diversity and destroying natural systems are the same people who are making policy decisions that will determine the future of life in America and elsewhere on Earth. An eco-justice curriculum should contribute to democratizing that decision-making process. The expert's approach to realizing the Western myth of material progress has led to the chemical contamination of much of the environment and food supply, the loss of employment resulting from technological innovations, and the global spread of the monoculture of consumerism. Decision making by marginalized cultural groups has been limited largely to protesting the adverse impacts of these changes on their lives. The educational goal now is to widen the circle of decision makers to include all the social groups affected by the decisions—even the groups once supported only by radical social critics. This goal is now endorsed by the American Association for the Advancement of Science, an organization that represents the views of mainstream science and technology practitioners. Following a recent symposium on what America's post–cold war science policy should be, the AAAS issued a report stating that "decisions on scientific and technical issues should incorporate input from affected communities and other members of the public, as many European nations have done" (1999:2). The report goes on to recommend that "Congress should examine alternative, community-based forms of research. Community-based research involves affected local communities in setting the research agenda and also in performing the research, and has proved successful in epidemiological and pollution research on local problems" (3). The successes of citizen participation in Denmark in recommending policies governing the introduction of genetically altered food and of citizen involvement in other European countries in democratizing science and technology policies were important influences shaping the AAAS recommendations. I mention this shift in the official position of the AAAS in order to emphasize the growing awareness that the democratic process is basic to addressing eco-justice issues. By extension, an eco-justice-centered curriculum is essential to ensuring that the various cultural groups affected by policy decisions possess the background knowledge they need to articulate their concerns and vital interests.

The challenge now is to envision the connection between education and a democratic polity in a way that is no longer based on the premise that the individual is the primary political unit. As I have explained elsewhere (Bowers 1995, 1997), the idea of the individual as an autonomous, rational being is an ideological construction based on the failure of earlier Western political theorists and philosophers to understand how languaging processes reproduce patterns of thought that have a distinct cultural history. Thus, the form of democracy to be strengthened by an eco-justice curriculum is one that recognizes individualized perspectives and talents as being embedded in distinct cultural approaches to community.

This awareness of interdependence across different symbolic and biological scales of existence goes well beyond Dewey's emphasis on connecting education to the community-centered process of participatory decision making. Dewey reflected the anthropocentric thinking of his era, but the process of decision making he equated with growth in reconstructing problematic experiences was based on a number of modern assumptions that negated the legitimacy of other cultural ways of knowing. As I have discussed this elsewhere (Bowers 1987, 1995, 1997), here I will only caution against the popular tendency to view Dewey as an early exponent of an eco-justice curriculum. Richard Rorty's *Contingency, Irony, and Solidarity* (1989) demonstrates how easily the more promising aspects of Dewey's thinking (e.g., his emphases on intelligence as social in nature and participatory decision making) can be overshadowed by the relativizing orientation of his epistemology. The "ironist individual" whom Rorty represents as the embodiment of Dewey's epistemology holds the following view: "To see one's language, one's conscience, one's morality, and one's highest hopes as contingent products, a literalization of what once were accidentally produced metaphors, is to adopt a self-identity which suits one for citizenship in such an ideally liberal state" (1989:61). In effect, everything is relative, and thus the ironist individual is involved in an ongoing process of political negotiation with other ironist individuals who also view all ideas, values, and norms as contingent. This naive and romantic view of a participatory democracy fails to account for how language-mediated thought continually brings a cultural perspective into the political process.

The anthropocentric foundations of Paulo Freire, as well as the modern assumptions he based his emancipatory pedagogy on, disqualify him from being an early exponent of an eco-justice curriculum. When the cultural epistemologies of non-Western cultures and the differences in relationships and thought patterns associated with print and oral forms of encoding and communicating are taken into account, it is difficult to see how Freire's emancipatory pedagogy could be interpreted as a universal panacea.

How an eco-justice curriculum differs from what educational theorists advocate, as examined in the earlier chapters, can best be understood by considering the background knowledge that students need to possess in order to exercise communicative competence within their communities. I use the word *understand* here not to mean a purely cognitive grasp of abstract relationships and issues. Rather, understanding encompasses an explicit understanding of relationships and processes, an embodied knowledge of community relationships and the ecology of place, and an awareness of the layered nature of the interdependencies of life-sustaining processes. The patterns of community life may, of course, reflect a mix of traditional ethnic influences and patterns dictated by an increasingly dependent consumer lifestyle.

Background Issues

The content of an eco-justice public school and university curriculum can, in part, be determined by assessing what students already understand (used here in the broadest sense of the word) about the characteristics of interdependent communities and the impact of these communities on natural systems. Do they recognize the skills, values, and theoretical and embodied knowledge they need to possess in order to participate in their primary community and in sustainable activities within local ecosystems? Are environmentally oriented courses educating them in ways that perpetuate the scientific and technological management approach to the environment, or are students being given the understanding and skills necessary for living less consumer-dependent lives?

The following represent a few of the questions that should be included in the assessment:

Who are the mentors in your home community and what do they contribute?

Who are the elders, and why are they important?

What are the networks of mutual aid?

What are the characteristics of a lifestyle based on the principles of voluntary simplicity?

How can the interdependence of rural and urban economies and ecologies be strengthened?

Which intergenerational skills and knowledge represent an alternative to meeting personal needs through consumerism?

What are the areas of community life in which a barter system can be utilized?

What is your community's source of fresh water, and where do the wastes go?

What are the patterns of animal migration in your bioregion?

What are the native plants and animals, and which are now threatened with extinction?

What features of the land are most likely to be affected by extreme weather conditions, and thus are unsafe to build on?

Are there narratives that contain wisdom about culture-nature relationships that were not understood by previous generations and still go unheeded today? What are they?

How have the experiences of place influenced your personal sense of identity and values?

Students' responses to these questions need to be considered in relation to how the distinction between high- and low-status knowledge affects racial, gender, and class relationships. The questions focus on aspects of community that public schools and universities generally designate low status, and thus not worthy of being included in the curriculum. Students' responses to these questions may also reveal the extent of the double bind in which social justice and even environmentally oriented programs of study reinforce the modern patterns of thinking that undermine the noncommodified aspects of community and perpetuate the cycle of environmental abuse.

An eco-justice curriculum should offer a critique of cultural patterns that privilege certain social groups over others and should provide conceptual and embodied understandings of how to participate in the process of renewing a more vital experience of community. It should also broaden the students' understanding of the impact of introducing changes into the environment that degrade the quality of human life—especially for those who occupy the economic and political margins of society. Examples of such eco-injustices are as numerous as the forms of environmental degradation they have caused. To cite a specific example that highlights the segment of society most affected by chemical contamination: the use of Roundup (a herbicide) has been linked to lung damage, nausea, reproductive problems, chromosome aberrations, and the destruction of red blood cells. The social group most affected by its use are the migrant farm workers and hourly wage-earners who apply it to crops, not the white-collar segment of society who purchase the fruits and vegetables in the supermarket.

Similarly, eco-justice issues are an integral aspect of new technologies, international treaties, and the continuing centralization of corporate power that leads to exporting jobs to regions of the world where wages are low and environmental regulations nearly nonexistent. The *maquiladoras* who experience the health consequences of the chemical contamination that stretches along the U.S.–Mexico border are not the only casualties of the southward flight of U.S. businesses. The workers on the U.S. side who have lost their jobs have also been victimized by a system that values profits above the health of the environment and its inhabitants. Perhaps the least recognized casualty of consumer society's relentless pursuit of technology is the intergenerational knowledge essential to sustaining cultural identities, networks of mutual support, and knowledge and skills not dependent on a monetized relationship. Indeed, each thematic area of an eco-justice curriculum needs to be viewed as addressing reforms vital to reconstituting the inter-generational community networks that have been undermined by the extreme imbalance that now exists between community and market forces.

Before identifying specific curriculum themes, I must address yet another background issue—namely, how educators can be expected to guide students in the examination of areas of culture that they themselves have not studied in any depth. A discussion of the distinction between high- and low-status knowledge may help us recognize the solution to the problem. As I explain in *The Culture of Denial,* high-status knowledge is based on a number of culturally specific assumptions and forms of cultural coding. Encoding knowledge in print, which makes it appear objective, is one of the primary characteristics of high-status knowledge. The assumption that individuals are autonomous in the sense of making up their *own* minds and having their *own* perspective on an external world is another. Low-status knowledge, which is a construct of formal educational institutions, includes such characteristics as non-commodified relationships and activities, face-to-face intergenerational communication, and patterns of mutual support and solidarity. That low-status knowledge is the basis of community life is particularly relevant to understanding how classroom teachers and university professors can overcome their own preconditioning in ways that help students recognize the everyday praxis of low-status knowledge.

What I am proposing here is a genuine possibility. That is, while teachers' indoctrination into high-status patterns of thinking will make it difficult to carry out the following recommendations, the shift in orientation that an eco-justice curriculum requires is not impossible. Resistance will come from high-status thinkers who continue to uphold the validity and explanatory power of culturally decontextualized theories. Scientists' claim that their approach to knowledge is free of cultural and personal influences is just one of many examples of how academics ignore how the language in which they think and communicate reproduces the deep conceptual categories of their language community. The long-standing tradition of anthropologists studying other cultures while ignoring the need to understand their own taken-for-granted cultural patterns (which is now beginning to change) is another. Other examples include the theories that explain the genetic basis of behavior, how the brain works, and the principles governing market decisions—all of which fail to consider the theorist's own cultural ecology.

This ability to ignore the patterns reenacted in immediate experience is partly a result of social conditioning. But there is also an element of personal denial that may be traced to issues surrounding personal and professional identity, peer approval, and the psychological gains that accompany identification with high-status knowledge. The main point here is that there are many cultural and psychological forces that work against our valuing the patterns of daily life. The success of an eco-justice curriculum will thus depend on the willingness of classroom teachers and university professors to use the patterns reenacted in daily experience as a basis for raising awareness of what is ecologically problematic in the high-status knowledge that constitutes the curriculum. The ability to explicate the patterns that contribute to morally coherent forms of community and to examine the patterns and technologies that undermine them is also a matter of choice.

While resistance to including in the curriculum the kind of knowledge and experiences suggested in the above assessment questions continues to be widespread, there has been a change in public attitude that cuts across the lines separating many cultural groups and social classes. This new attitude strongly suggests that there would now be widespread community support for an eco-justice curriculum. In particular, there is a growing awareness that the media, the profit motive, and corporate control are overwhelming nonmaterial community sources of identity formation and values. This awareness even led the editors of *Business Week* (a traditional advocate of corporate interests) to publish an article titled "The All-out Marketing Assault on Your Child's Heart, Mind, and Wallet" (Wechsler 1997:62–69). The new attitude makes possible the use of the cultural resources of local communities as an integral part of an eco-justice curriculum. The implementation of such a curriculum is still contingent, however, on the ability of educators to contribute to renewing the noncommodified relations and activities within local communities, and in the process to help students understand the unresolved equity and eco-justice issues.

Thematic Areas in an Eco-Justice Curriculum

The cultural patterns shared within a language community generally are learned and reenacted at a taken-for-granted level of awareness. That is, most of the cultural patterns that are the source of shared meanings—and thus are the basis of reciprocal actions—represent a stock of tacit knowledge that comes into play in context-specific ways. Most individuals, regardless of their cultural membership, are unaware of how their behaviors, values, and interpretations are influenced by widely shared cultural patterns. The dominant Western culture's emphasis on autonomous individuals as the basic social unit further undermines the ability to be explicitly aware of these tacitly held patterns. What is important about this tacit and contextual knowledge is that it can be made explicit through the use of language. That is, giving students the language that names the relationships and behaviors is the first step toward making the patterns explicit—which, in turn, is the first step in politicizing the patterns. The power of language both to hide and to reveal can be seen in how the tacit understandings encoded in language have sustained gender and ethnic biases over centuries— even as people claimed to be rational and self-directing. The explicit naming of the patterns brought them to the level of awareness, which then made it possible to recognize the social justice issues that needed to be addressed. This process of naming the relationships and behaviors in ways that make them explicit is a key aspect of an eco-justice curriculum. But it should not be assumed that critical awareness automatically leads to progressive change. The naming process must also take into account an issue largely ignored by social justice theorists: namely, the need for an intergenerational accountability that renews the genuine achievements of the past in ways that do not diminish the prospects of future generations. It is this sense of balance between fostering critical awareness and affirming what is positive and life sustaining (which will vary according to the traditions of the cultural group) that separates an eco-justice curriculum from approaches taken by critical pedagogy theorists and educational reformers who base their recommendations on romantic assumptions about the self-organizing characteristics inherent in all individual experience and natural systems.

Below I discuss several of the themes important to an eco-justice pedagogy. Each of the themes should be introduced in the early grades in order to ensure that students' conceptual "maps" take account of the "territory" of daily experience—to use Gregory Bateson's metaphors. The lived cultural patterns and relationships encompassed by these themes should be considered an integral part of the curriculum at all levels of the educational process. Adding conceptual and experiential depth to the theme as the student advances through the grades ensures that it does not become reduced to an isolated segment of the curriculum that is dealt with in an abstract way. Helping students recognize and articulate the ways that different cultural patterns influence relationships requires the ability to make explicit the patterns of everyday life and knowledge of which questions to ask about the relationships they make possible. Teaching students different explanatory frameworks, the history of ideas, and how different cultures developed will frame the discussion in ways that enable them to recognize the connections between the cultural patterns they might otherwise take for granted and the technological changes taking place in the world.

Commodification

One of the most dynamic and disruptive characteristics of modern culture is its tendency to commodify knowledge, relationships, and skills. Indeed, one of the hallmarks of modernization has been the shift in market relationships from a peripheral though essential aspect of community life to the dominant focal point of human interaction. There are now few aspects of modern life that have not been commodified—even tragedies and simulated violence are being used to bolster the media ratings necessary to generate profits for advertisers. The pervasiveness of market-oriented relationships in the earliest years of childhood can be seen in the emphasis on clothes, entertainment, food, and health care. The use of computers as a substitute for what was previously learned through face-to-face communication—storytelling, play, and problem solving—extends the commodification process to even earlier stages in the child's development. The culture of commodification now encompasses every aspect of adults' lives as well: sexual reproduction, health care, leisure activities, spiritual growth, and death itself. The impact of commodification on indigenous groups can be seen in the displacement of traditional knowledge and values by television and video games. Youth captivated by mainstream cultural icons such as Michael Jordan, Nike, and the Denver Broncos are becoming increasingly alienated from the subsistence knowledge of the older generation. And with the development of biotechnology and recent court decisions that allow corporations to patent and thus own gene lines like private property, commodification has been extended in ways that go far beyond the earlier practice of treating Nature as a "natural resource."

Science and technology are not inherently destructive. The process of using new knowledge to create products and services has been an aspect of human existence for thousands of years. The problem lies with the extent to which it has taken over human relationships and altered people's values. Of specific concern is the way the relentless expansion of the culture of commodification creates an ever-expanding list of human needs and a dependency on consumerism as a way of meeting them. As Ivan Illich pointed out several decades ago, this dependency is the source of poverty when it leads to the loss of skills necessary for self-reliance and networks of mutual aid. An example duplicated in many parts of North America is the situation of the Gwich'in—an indigenous culture that inhabits 1.8 million acres of what was once a fenceless, wireless, and uncontaminated expanse of the Alaskan tundra. Before television brought the message that real food comes in cans, clothes carry logos, and travel requires a four-wheel-drive vehicle, the Gwich'in relied solely on caribou hunting to meet their needs for food, clothes, shelter, and ceremonies. Today, the youth of the villages sit in front of the television dreaming of becoming professional football players and playing video games while the knowledge that previously enabled the Gwich'in to be self-sufficient seeps away. Their survival now depends on government "subsistence" checks, food stamps, and store-bought commodities.

The same process of consumer dependency is reenacted in middle-class families in which restaurants and fast food outlets have replaced intergenerational knowledge of how to grow, preserve, and prepare food.

The other major problem connected with the commodification of every aspect of cultural life, and Nature itself, is that it contributes to the cycle of degrading ecosystems by extracting the "resources" necessary for the production of consumer items—which are shortly returned to Nature as waste. If the rest of the world shared North America's level of consumerism, two additional planets would be required to produce the resources and absorb the waste (Wackernagel and Rees 1996:15).

Gerald Berthoud has suggested a way in which lessons about the dynamics and effects of the commodification process can be introduced into the curriculum. In his essay "Market" he summarizes the transition from markets held on a specific day and location in the community to marketplaces so pervasive that many people today cannot imagine examples of noncommodified activities and relationships. "We are all subject to the compelling idea that everything that can be made must be made and sold," he writes. "Our universe appears unshakably structured by the omnipotence of technoscientific truth and the laws of the market" (1992:71). The chief question raised by his observation is: Are there any aspects of individual and community experience that have not been commodified and calculated as part of the gross domestic product? This question can be used by teachers from elementary grades through graduate school as the starting point for an examination of alternatives to the symbolic infrastructure that supports globalized commodification.

The question is important for a number of reasons that have curricular significance. For one, it focuses attention on those aspects of human experience that have not yet been integrated into the market. It also focuses attention on how different cultural groups have been able to limit the spread of commodification—as well as how they have been transformed by it. A discussion of the fundamental differences at the level of daily experience between commodified and noncommodified activities can then lead to a cultural survey of local communities, with the focus on activities that are not mainly dependent on consumerism. This survey will provide both a basis for recognizing the extent to which skills are being replaced by a dependence on the possibilities encoded in consumer products and a basis for recognizing the existing possibilities within communities for engaging in noncommodified relationships and activities. In effect, the cultural survey will bring to the students' attention the different activities, mentoring relationships, and skills still being shared within the community—which may range from theater and musical groups to soccer clubs, gardening, and house restoration projects.

Teachers in the early grades should introduce the basic distinction between commodified and noncommodified activities by having students describe the difference between play based on face-to-face relationships and play that is largely dictated by the design characteristics of purchased toys. Young students can also be encouraged to discuss the differences between embodied learning in the natural environment and visual (television) and print-based (computers) forms of learning. The differences between meals prepared in the home according to recipes handed down through the generations and the assembly-line production at the local fast food outlet can also be part of the process of sorting out the transforming effects of the commodification process. Young students are very perceptive about differences in their experiences, but it seldom occurs to teachers to legitimize the importance of articulating the nature of these differences—and over time, they may cease to be noticeable.

As students acquire a wider range of experience and depth of understanding, the historical roots of commodification (including the formation of the guiding ideology) can be introduced. If students are not told of the widespread use of the barter system before work and "products" were monetized, for example, they are less likely to understand how the reintroduction of bartering and even the use of a local currency can lead to the regeneration of more self-reliant communities. For example, the use of local currency, which has become known as local exchange trading systems, or LETS, has spread to communities in Canada, Australia, Great Britain, and the United States. Similarly, if students are left unaware of alternative pathways of personal development that can be attained in mentoring relationships, as well as the historical importance of mentoring, the allure of commodified culture will likely dominate their experience.

Older students should be encouraged to examine the differences between the ecological footprint left by community-based activities and relationships and those based on consumerism. This line of inquiry needs to be supplemented by examining the drive to create global markets and the loss of local knowledge and self-sufficient practices; the ecological consequences of a world monoculture centered on Western-style consumerism; Western ideologies (Marxism, socialism, and various genres of liberalism and conservatism) that strengthen or provide genuine alternatives to the spread of a consumer-oriented culture; and the ways the commodification process is reinforced through the use of computer-enhanced art, sex and violence, and modern mythic images of what constitutes success and power.

Obviously, the latter topics can be examined in depth only when students reach high school and university levels of critical understanding. But the study of the cultural and ecological consequences of commodification at all levels, even the earliest stages of the students' education, should be accompanied by a far-reaching assessment of noncommodified forms of activities and relationships and discussions of how different cultural groups renew them.

Traditions

Cultural traditions are reenacted and individually interpreted in every aspect of daily life—even in the daily experiences of supposedly radical theorists who claim that emancipation can be achieved only by overturning all traditions. Freire, for example, claims that we "should understand life, not necessarily as the daily repetition of things, but as an effort to create and re-create, and as an effort to rebel, as well" (1985:199). Freire once visited Portland State University, where we shared a most edifying lunch. The topics and patterns of our conversation involved reliance on traditions, which he characterized as outmoded patterns that limit the creative possibilities of experience. If he had acted consistently with his ideologically driven misrepresentation of tradition, however, he would have had to create, in Prigogine-Whitehead fashion, new technologies for traveling to Portland, new patterns of metacommunication during his debate with me, new technologies for preparing the meal, and even the clothes we were wearing.

As I pointed out earlier, *tradition* is an iconic metaphor that encodes Enlightenment thinkers' association of that term with a number of genuinely unjust relationships and practices rooted in feudal society. These earlier thinkers did not associate the word with *all* the cultural patterns and practices that survive over enough generations to become part of the taken-for-granted stock of cultural knowledge. When tradition is understood as synonymous with this whole range of beliefs and practices, however, from the spelling of words and use of capitalization to legal, technological, and religious traditions, it then becomes more obvious that *tradi-*

tion designates the entire scope and continuity of cultural practices. As students from the earliest grades through graduate school reenact traditions in every aspect of their lives, these patterns and practices should be viewed as an essential area of study in an experientially grounded, ecologically oriented curriculum.

Because many social justice theorists wrongly associate tradition only with patterns of discrimination and domination, it is important here to emphasize that a more complex and balanced understanding of tradition is essential. If we could live without traditions, as advocated by critical pedagogy theorists and assumed to be a possibility by the followers of Prigogine and Whitehead, there would be no community—just individuals engaged in critical reflection and an endless search for new forms of creative expression. Aspects of community such as mentoring, sharing of intergenerational knowledge and skills along with languaging patterns, the networks of mutual support and protocols governing moral reciprocity, and narratives that bond the present with past and future generations are all examples of tradition.

That not all traditions contribute to socially and ecologically just communities makes it even more imperative that students be encouraged from the earliest grades to examine the range of traditions reenacted in everyday life. The inclusion of tradition as a theme in an eco-justice curriculum is yet another way of making students aware of patterns and activities so integral to the unconscious ways of thinking and doing that they go unrecognized.

The cultural survey of traditions enacted by students in the earliest grades will help counter the erroneous conceptual framework reinforced by the media and in popular discourse that represents change and innovation as the expression of progress. Even at this early stage of education, students can be encouraged to name (that is, make explicit) how they experience different forms of tradition. For example, they can examine the gains and losses in personal experience that accompany the reenactment of patterns of nonverbal communication, ceremonies, rules, and institutionalized procedures that protect their individual rights—including the assumption that one is presumed innocent until proven guilty. Students in the early grades can also understand, if the distinction is clarified for them, the difference between a fad and a tradition—as both are part of their daily experience.

More advanced study of cultural continuities (traditions) should lead to the examination of the ideological roots of widely held misconceptions about the nature of tradition—such as the assumption that traditions are static and are obstacles to change and innovation. Students should also be encouraged to study how ideological misrepresentations are encoded in the metaphors that reproduce older analogies that serve as the conceptual framework for understanding in the present. An eco-justice curriculum should also provide for the critical study of the nature of the antitradition traditions at the core of modern societies—and who gains and loses from promoting them. This analysis will bring out a dimension of science, emancipatory educational and social theories, and techno-utopian thinking that is seldom considered. Sorting out the gains and losses, particularly as they relate to the need to strengthen the non-consumer-dependent patterns of social relationships, can take students in many directions—especially when it is understood that modern technologies are given moral legitimacy by the traditions of liberal thought. Understanding science as an example of an antitradition would help students recognize both the benefits of scientific discoveries and how the epistemology of science is complicit in the development of many environmentally destructive technologies.

The study of tradition as a cultural phenomenon should include an examination of the most fundamental questions that now face humanity: How does replacing the traditions of other cultural groups with the antitradition traditions of Western modernism affect their prospects of ecological survival? Can we achieve a greater degree of eco-justice if we rely more on the political process of negotiated agreements than on the traditions of moral insights encoded in narratives, sacred texts, and the experience of moral relationships accumulated over hundreds, even thousands, of years? Is there a double bind in valuing cultural diversity while denying the importance of intergenerational traditions—and urging the children of these different cultural groups to adopt the deep cultural assumptions that underlie an emancipatory approach to education? What are the most valued traditions that impede the realization of more just human and environmental relationships?

These are weighty questions that do not lend themselves to the formulaic answers found in modern ideologies. There is, however, a lighter and more activity-oriented dimension to the study of tradition. This includes the noncommodified traditions that students might want to experience for themselves, ranging from sports, music, theater, and nature study to gardening, volunteerism, and learning a craft. As different communities often have a mix of cultural traditions, the possibilities of student involvement will be fully disclosed only through a survey of the traditions being sustained in the community. As suggested earlier, this survey should be part of the curriculum.

Technology

From the earliest grades through graduate school, students experience the mediating influence of technology on their personal experience—as the background noise of their controlled environment, as switches and other technological objects that are manipulated, and as a source of mediation that amplifies and reduces cultural and personal dimensions of experience. In short, technology has largely displaced natural phenomena as the primary context of the student's experience. In the past, when the development of more efficient technologies was considered less important than the development of the skill and judgment of the person making them, technologies played a negligible role in the lives of individuals and cultural groups. Today, however, technology is characterized by a number of double binds that combine important benefits with risks to people's—and entire populations'—health and self-sufficiency. Among the many examples that demonstrate that equal access to the use of a modern technology may not be sufficient to rectify deeper eco-justice issues is the fate of the more than two million Mexican small landowners who can no longer compete with the technology of North American farmers. A second example is the even greater threat to the world's food supply posed by genetically engineered seeds that make small-scale farmers in the South increasingly dependent on corporate giants. In short, modern technology is now the greatest obstacle to development along ecologically sustainable pathways. Yet, the study of the implications of technology is largely neglected in the curriculum of the public schools and universities.

Complex eco-justice issues surround nearly every major area of modern technological development. The emerging field of biotechnology, which has given us recombinant Bovine Growth Hormone to increase milk production and Roundup-Ready soy and cotton (to cite just a few examples), raises a wide range of health and food supply issues. In addition, there are the eco-justice issues surrounding the culture-mediating characteristics of computers that were discussed in Chapter 3. The continuing drive to create technologies that will further de-skill workers and displace small-scale producers with integrated corporate giants raises another set of eco-justice issues. If we are to heed the advice of Richard Sclove, and others, on the need to democratize the process of technological innovation, it will be necessary to use the curriculum to provide the conceptual basis for recognizing the connections between modern technologies and eco-justice issues.

The basic insight that technology is not a neutral tool can be introduced in the earliest grades in ways that draw on students' personal experiences and ability to articulate how they have already learned to think about technology. Like the other themes in an eco-justice curriculum, the level of analysis can be deepened and broadened through the introduction of theories that illuminate relationships not likely to be understood in the earlier grades. The recommendation here is not to create a specific curriculum unit or course that examines the characteristics of and issues associated with modern technology. Rather, the analysis should be part of every aspect of the curriculum—in the arts, sciences, history, literature, and so forth.

Depending on the maturity of the student, inquiry about the constructive and destructive effects of technology can be organized around the following questions.

How has the language that organizes our thought patterns been influenced by technology? Students in the early grades can be encouraged to pay attention to words and thought patterns (analogies) that have been derived from technology. Older students should study how the language of technology that privileges certain groups over others is based on powerful metanarratives and undermines ways of thinking that are not part of the industrial mindset.

Does the technology allow for further development of the skill and insight of the user? Younger students can examine the issue of skill development by comparing their own ability to do cursive writing and drawings with the mechanistic process and seemingly wider range of choices made available by computers. This particular aspect of student experience can lead to the discussion of issues not likely to be addressed in any other setting. How the value of individual skill is sacrificed to the values of efficiency and machine standardization in the dominant culture can be compared with non-Western cultures' emphasis on the development of personal skills, aesthetic judgment, and social usefulness.

How do different forms of technology influence the relationships between people and those between cultural groups? The ways print and computer-mediated communication change relationships in fundamental ways should be examined here. These technologies, which are part of even the youngest middle-class child's experience, can be the starting point for making explicit the patterns that would, in most instances, be a taken-for-granted part of daily experience. How other technologies, such as the automobile and biotechnology, influence intergenerational and community relationships should be considered in later grades.

How do different forms of technology influence the patterns of control existing within different cultural groups—and between cultural groups? Do they undermine the noncommodified patterns of families and communities by creating new forms of dependency? Are these dependencies part of a network of control that benefits certain groups at the expense of others? How does the use of different technologies influence the process of socialization? Do they strengthen or undermine the community of memory and moral reciprocity? Which technologies and legitimating ideologies contribute to the form of extreme self-centered subjectivity that leads to viewing values and other group norms as relative to the judgment of the individual?

Does the technology reflect an industrial pattern of thinking or does it incorporate what Sim Van Der Ryn and Stuart Cowan refer to as the principles of ecological design? Each of the principles of ecological design (solutions grow from place, ecological accounting informs design, design with nature, everyone is a designer, and make nature visible [Van Der Ryn and Cowan 1996:54–56]) leads to the study of different technologies contextualized in terms of the students' understanding of their bioregion, community traditions, and unresolved eco-justice issues. The differences between technology based on an industrial pattern of thinking and the principles of ecological design can be easily recognized in the computer simulation program *SimCity*, which is widely used in public schools.

Of all the questions about the eco-justice implications of different forms of technology, the only one that is not fully dependent on making explicit how technology mediates the direct experience of the student is the one dealing with the difference between the industrial and ecological design of technology. Exploration of the other questions can begin by making explicit the otherwise taken-for-granted patterns and relationships of daily experience. Bringing a comparative cultural perspective to the discussion is also essential, and is made relatively easy by the different cultural perspectives that are already present in the typical North American classroom.

If teachers are to help students understand the historical forces that influenced the development of different technologies, they must engage in a more systematic study of technology as part of their own university education. On their own, however, teachers are not likely to read the works of Jacques Ellul, Lewis Mumford, Langdon Winner, Theodore Roszak, or any of the other major thinkers in this area. Unfortunately, the issue of reform in this area of university education is beyond the scope of this book.

Science

Contrary to the widespread understanding, science is part of the double bind that is accelerating the degradation of natural systems. The way science is currently taught in public schools and universities fails to address its role in contributing to the globalization of the more ecologically problematic aspects of the modern mindset.

This criticism is made with the full recognition of the many contributions that Western science has made to improving the quality of human life. The problem in the current approach to teaching science is that it presents only the positive contributions. How science, as a culturally specific way of knowing, contributes to the delegitimation of the mythopoetic narratives of non-Western cultures while promoting the metanarrative of evolution (which equates survival with Darwinian fitness) is not part of the curriculum. Nor does it include moral issues such as those generated, for example, by scientists working on weapons systems and in the field of biotechnology. That scientists willingly worked on a Monsanto project to create a toxin-producing gene that would have forced poor farmers to depend on purchased seeds for the next year's planting should lead any thinking person to question the wisdom of treating education in the sciences as entirely separate from moral issues.

Science teachers must be taught to recognize both the positive and the negative aspects of science. We have gained from science in our increased capacity to explain, predict, and control certain aspects of natural phenomena. But these gains have advanced the Industrial Revolution—to which computer technology is giving new life and energy. The Industrial Revolution, especially since World War II, has introduced tens of thousands of synthetic chemicals into the environment. The rationale for doing so has always been couched in terms of contributing to human progress and advancing scientific knowledge. The authors of *Our Stolen Future: Are We Threatening Our Fertility, Intelligence, and Survival?* (1996) explain the seriousness of the double bind in the following way:

> Over the past fifty years, synthetic chemicals have become so pervasive in the environment and in our bodies that it is no longer possible to define a normal, unaltered human physiology. There is no clean, uncontaminated place, nor any human being who hasn't acquired

a considerable load of persistent hormone-disrupting chemicals.
In this experiment, we are all guinea pigs and, to make matters
worse, we have no controls to help us understand what these chemicals are doing. . . . It is no longer sufficient to look for the next round
of substitutes for existing chemicals, for a new generation of supposedly less damaging synthetic compounds. The time has come to
shift the discussion to the global experiment itself. (Colburn et al.
1996: 240–241)

The title of the book foregrounds critical eco-justice issues that go
beyond the valid critiques of science now being made from feminist
and ethnic perspectives.

So the crucial questions become: How does an eco-justice curriculum present a balanced view of science—its achievements *and*
its inappropriate uses? How do we provide the conceptual and
moral basis for democratizing the use of science? And, more important, how do we change scientists' taken-for-granted patterns of
thinking? How do we convince them that science is not based on a
culturally neutral mode of inquiry and that they are morally accountable for how their research is turned into technologies that
disrupt the lives of people and put their health at risk? The answers
to these questions, in part, will be settled by the emergence of a new
mythopoetic narrative and the regeneration of older ones that rees-
tablish a taken-for-granted understanding of the moral nature of
relationships—between different cultural groups and between humans and the natural environment. These new mythopoetic narratives will make unthinkable the scientific challenge of cloning a human being; the replacement of humans by computers as advocated
by Moravec, Kurzweil, and other scientists; and the biotechnologies
that are altering the genetic basis of life in order to increase corporate profits. Public schools and universities cannot create new narratives, but they can promote the process by including in the curriculum a more culturally complex view of science.

Even very young students should be taught that scientists think in culturally specific patterns. They must understand that scientists share a linear view of progress with the dominant culture, emphasize the separation of objective knowledge from moral values, and too often disregard how the cultural language processes in which they are embedded organize their thought processes. These are complex issues to raise, but even in the earliest grades it is possible to point out the cultural assumptions that are part of the science lesson. Presenting examples of how indigenous cultures integrate within their moral systems what is learned from careful observation will help even the youngest students recognize that Western science is guided by assumptions that often undermine the moral values of local groups. For example, the ceremonies practiced by indigenous cultures in the Pacific Northwest to celebrate the return of the salmon not only renewed the sacred bond between the people and a cycle of Nature, they also allowed large numbers of salmon to migrate upstream without interference. The Hopi ceremonies surrounding the planting of corn represent yet another example of how a moral/spiritual way of understanding enabled a culture to adapt their agricultural knowledge to the characteristics of their bioregion. By way of contrast, anthropologists' long-standing practice of exhuming bodies from indigenous burial sites for the purpose of scientific study is one of many examples of the search for new knowledge taking precedence over other values—including what is held to be sacred.

The history of scientific thought should be introduced in the later grades. Topics should include the systematic exclusion of women from science; the role of science in furthering the globalization of an industrial, consumer-oriented lifestyle; the connections between the different genres of liberalism and the ideology of science that justifies the domination of other cultural groups; the implications of the evolution metanarrative for justifying the global-

ization of the Western model of economic and technological development; and the misrepresentation of the scientific achievements
of non-Western cultures. Understanding that science is a cultural
phenomenon and that an informed public must accept responsibility for the cultural uses of science will help to counter the claims of
some prominent scientists (who seem to be at odds with the
AAAS) that only scientists are qualified to make judgments about
the uses of scientific knowledge. The tendency to frame social justice issues in terms of equality of opportunity to pursue scientific
careers (which is indeed a legitimate concern of feminist and ethnic
groups) needs to be broadened to include an understanding of how
the darker side of science is often at the roots of eco-justice issues.

Language

Every aspect of culture can be understood as part of an ecology of
symbols that communicate and sustain the patterns, norms, and
relationships reenacted in everyday life—even as they are given individualistic interpretation. That is, the symbol systems in nonverbal communication, architecture, clothes, and the design of technologies are all part of the languaging processes that mediate
relationships, values, and understandings. Because the languaging
processes are as broad and complex as the culture, it is necessary to
be specific about which aspects should be included in an eco-justice
curriculum.

Like the other themes in an eco-justice curriculum, the languaging processes are not an abstraction. Rather, they are integral
to the context of the students' immediate and embodied experience. The environment of the young child (regardless of class, gender, and ethnicity) is an ecology of patterns communicated through
multiple interactions with others and through the thought patterns
encoded in the material expressions of culture. The symbolic ecol-

ogy of the more widely socialized individual is no less influential in sustaining the shared cultural patterns—even when the individual moves between the languaging processes of different cultural groups. Thus, the content of this aspect of an eco-justice curriculum is always part of the immediate experience of the student. The relevant eco-justice issues that should be examined will depend on the students' level of understanding and experience and on the teacher's ability to recognize how different languaging processes reproduce patterns that are destructive of community and the natural environment. As most cultural patterns are learned and reenacted at the taken-for-granted level of awareness, teachers, like everyone else, are generally unaware of the languaging patterns embedded in the curriculum. That is, while teachers focus on the explicit curriculum, or even the curriculum that comes into existence through the self-organizing activities of the students, the tacit curriculum of taken-for-granted cultural patterns continues to influence how everyday reality is experienced and acted out.

Given the often unrecognized nature of how the languaging processes influence awareness and behavior, a number of specific aspects of languaging processes can be gradually introduced. These include the following.

Understanding that languaging processes reproduce the shared patterns that are the source of meaning and understanding of relationships and moral norms, and are integral to how self-identity is formed and experienced. A focus on the shared patterns in the different languaging processes makes it easier to recognize how much of experience involves the reenactment of cultural patterns constituted in the past. This understanding then opens the door to a consideration of how these patterns encode deeply held assumptions and whether or not these patterns are ecologically and morally problematic.

Students must understand another aspect of language as well.

Indeed, it is an aspect of language not understood by the followers of Dewey, Freire, Prigogine, and Whitehead. Cultural languages not only encode the patterns that need to be made explicit and reconstituted, they also encode understandings and moral norms accumulated over generations of living within a specific bioregion. The languages of cultural groups are storehouses of knowledge of the characteristics of local plants and animals, weather patterns, and the integration of ceremonies with the natural cycles within the bioregion. Linguists now estimate that half of the world's six thousand spoken languages will die out in the next century, and only 5 percent are likely to survive over the long term. In effect, linguists are predicting a radical narrowing of cultural diversity. Environmentalists warn that with this loss of cultural diversity we will lose vital knowledge of how to live within the limitations of different bioregions. This connection between languages, cultural diversity, and knowledge of local ecosystems also needs to be integrated into any discussion of how languaging and individual interpretation carry forward the taken-for-granted patterns that govern relationships.

Understanding that language is not a conduit in a sender-receiver process of communication. Rather, language encodes the metaphorical patterns of thought that were constituted in an earlier period of the cultural group's development. The ways spoken and printed words, the design of buildings and other technologies, and the values that influence relationships are based on a complex layering of metaphorical thinking are discussed in Chapter 5. The main point here is that an eco-justice curriculum should foster a greater awareness that language systems do not work as conduits through which individuals send their ideas to others. Rather, earlier metaphorical thinking, which often represented efforts to understand new situations, is reproduced through the use of language systems in ways that influence present ways of understanding and problem solving.

The prevailing analogues encoded in the iconic metaphors carry forward the dominant cultural group's taken-for-granted patterns of thinking. For example, the iconic metaphors that encoded analogues unchallenged for centuries in Western cultures continued until very recently to frame how the attributes of women and ethnic groups were understood. Historically rooted analogues for the environment as a natural resource, tradition as a barrier to progress, and community as limited to human relationships continue to provide taken-for-granted ways of thinking that still go unchallenged in most classrooms.

If students are to understand how languaging processes can undermine the development of morally coherent and ecologically sustainable communities, they must first understand (and recognize) the root metaphors that influence the process of analogic thinking and know how the prevailing analogues are reproduced in iconic metaphors such as *data, individualism, emancipation,* and *environment.* Students also need to understand the metaphorical constructions, including root metaphors, that continue to undermine eco-justice relationships and lifestyles. For example, students should be able to recognize the root metaphors and metanarratives that represent humans as dependent on changes occurring in natural systems and the root metaphors that foreground the moral rather than the economic basis of human relationships. An understanding of what contributes to viable communities—which may vary between ethnic groups—is required to understand the problems that languaging processes may generate.

Examples of the layered and culturally specific nature of metaphorical thinking are an integral aspect of every classroom—in the use of the spoken and printed word, in patterns of metacommunication, in clothes, and even in the technologies that students interact with. The omission of this aspect of culture from the curriculum can be traced directly to teachers' lack of understanding and to the failure of the university curriculum.

Understanding how the nonverbal and print-based message systems of the dominant culture exert a powerful influence in shaping the students' identity, expectations, and values. The influence of computer-enhanced images in media advertising and in the entertainment industry is becoming more widely recognized, although this recognition has not in any way modified efforts to use the media to foster even higher levels of consumerism. Recommendations for including media literacy in the curriculum need to be taken more seriously. In addition to recognizing how television and other electronic media influence consciousness, it is also important that students be able to decode the false messages conveyed in displays of consumer items in shopping malls and supermarkets. The visual message surrounding the presentation of consumer items is that of plenitude, technological control, and what successful people expect as a normal part of life. The design of the sport utility vehicle is yet another example of a cultural message system that needs to be decoded, as are the trophy homes that incorporate bad architectural design and features that encourage excessive consumption—such as the three-car garage. Hidden by the mesmerizing media images that sustain hyperconsumerism is its impact on the environment, and thus the quality of life of future generations.

Whether or not the ability to decode the many ways in which consumerism devastates the environment and undermines less materially oriented communities will lead students to adopt a less consumer-centered lifestyle is difficult to predict. When there are few cultural message systems that reinforce the importance of nonconsumer relationships, it is unfair to expect students not to want what most adults equate with happiness and success. But the possibility of change depends on an awareness of how the assumptions of the dominant culture are manifested in everyday life and the consequences of not resisting them. The ubiquitous electronic commerce and Wal-Mart-style megastores are simply the latest manifestation of the modern myths that need to be challenged.

With giant corporations such as Disney, General Electric, Time Warner, and Rupert Murdoch's News Corporation controlling nearly all avenues of public communication, an eco-justice curriculum is one of the few sites where students can develop the communicative competence they will need to address the double binds that characterize the dominant culture's emphasis on economic and technological growth.

5 The Practice of an Eco-Justice Pedagogy

What is the basic relationship of teacher and students when the curriculum is organized in ways that address eco-justice issues? How does an eco-justice pedagogy translate into classroom practices? The answers to these questions must be sought in the nature of the cultural and ecological changes now occurring on a worldwide scale. For example, the latest developments in the digital phase of the Industrial Revolution are evident in the spread of electronic commerce, further standardization of the production process, global marketing of everything from fast food to entertainment, and the globalization of the Cartesian form of consciousness and self-identity. The increase in world population coupled with a decline in major life-sustaining ecosystems (forest cover, fisheries, sources of fresh water, species diversity, etc.) is leading to a further degradation of the environment and worsening the plight of already marginalized cultural groups. The changes occurring as a result of global warming—increased frequency of El Niño and La Niña weather systems, tornadoes and hurricanes, a 40 percent reduction in the Arctic icecap, and a shift northward of tropical diseases, to cite just a few—are affecting people's lives in terms of direct physical dangers, the cost of protecting and rebuilding their homes, and in threats to their livelihood. Global warming and the climatic changes it is generating can largely be attributed to the globalization of Western technologies, including biotechnology, that are changing the chemistry of the Earth's natural systems—living and inanimate.

Attempts by individuals, communities, and countries to halt or reverse these environmental changes are often thwarted by the World Trade Organization, whose primary goal is to overturn any community, state, or national effort to protect the rights of workers and the environment that can be interpreted as restricting free trade. World Trade Organization agreements cover every field of economic endeavor, including agriculture, textiles, banking, telecommunications, industrial standards, and intellectual property. In effect, the organization's goal is to free corporations from restrictions that arise from efforts to protect local and national traditions essential to economic self-reliance and cultural identity.

This overview of changes now occurring on a global scale is not meant to create an immobilizing state of pessimism about the future. Rather, it is intended to provide a sense of realism and urgency about events that are beginning to affect every aspect of peoples' lives—from the state of their health and prospects for meaningful employment to the quality of their relationships with others and their sense of spiritual identity and renewal. Western technologies have made genuine contributions to the quality of human life, but these have been accompanied by double binds that we are only just now beginning to recognize. The current Disney mentality of using technology to maintain visual images that equate consumerism with progress, plenitude, and happiness helps many people remain in a state of self-denial about the nature of the environmental crisis. Corporate control of the media, along with the reductionism inherent in the thirty-second news bite, further ensures that the public will be exposed to a superficial level of understanding—and thus be unable to discriminate between the trivial and the politically significant.

The alarming changes in weather patterns and other natural systems noted above foreground two points that need to be considered in thinking about an eco-justice style of teaching. The first is that dissipative structures, process-oriented teaching, a single-minded focus on emancipation, and current teaching fads based on "constructivism," eight forms of intelligence, and multiculturalism are all based on the same deep cultural assumptions that provide the conceptual and moral legitimacy for the globalizing processes described above. To reiterate: to view change as the expression of linear progress, the individual as an autonomous decision maker, and the world as human-centered—the assumptions basic to the above interpretations of the purpose and role of the teacher—is to espouse the family of ideas and values that coevolved with the Industrial Revolution. The other point related to an eco-justice pedagogy is that the style of teaching, including decisions regarding the curriculum, must balance critical reflection with the renewal of community-centered traditions that represent an alternative to cultural trends that are now overshooting the long-term sustaining capacity of the environment.

When we consider the diversity of cultural ways of knowing, as well as the widely shared cultural patterns reenacted in such activities as education, sports, entertainment, politics, business, and community ceremonies, knowing when to change and when to renew and strengthen taken-for-granted patterns and practices becomes an especially daunting problem. Students from homes that maintain cultural traditions—whether they be Cajun, Latino, Asian American, Islamic, African American, Mong, Lakota, Diné/Navajo, or Western Apache—are a valuable resource but further magnify the challenge of knowing when to foster the critical awareness that relativizes the foundations of beliefs and values. Critical thought strengthens the modern form of subjective judgment and leads to politicizing the symbolic basis of relationships within a culture. Modern thinkers' tendency to equate the politicizing process with progressive change has prevented them from considering other approaches to reform, and thus what constitutes the appropriate domains for the Western model of emancipatory politics. As I pointed out earlier, there are times when critical reflection is necessary in order to eliminate oppressive practices handed down from the past, and times when fostering the form of individualism that accompanies critical thought becomes a matter of cultural domination, as Esteva and Prakash point out in *Grassroots Post-modernism* (1998). The myth of progress hides the complexity of the teacher's role in mediating how cultural practices and beliefs are passed on. Too often the myth has helped turn teaching into a set of ideologically driven techniques. Indeed, if the educational theories examined in earlier chapters are carefully considered, it becomes obvious that they are all process oriented. That is, they offer different techniques but little guidance about the actual content of the curriculum that is relevant to different cultural groups. Nor do they specify which beliefs and practices of different cultural groups contribute to eco-justice in community and environmental relationships. Unlike these other approaches, an eco-justice pedagogy cannot be reduced to a specific set of techniques, nor can it be assigned the mission of transforming all cultural groups by turning youth against the traditions of their parents and community.

In *The Culture of Denial* I argue that our educational institutions have relegated to low status some forms of knowledge that represent the patterns and relationships within communities that are not dependent on consumerism and expert systems. I also argue that educating (indoctrinating) students to think in the patterns of high-status knowledge is teaching them to interpret other cultural patterns of thinking as backward and ignorant. Thus, the challenge for the teacher who practices an eco-justice pedagogy will be to overcome the modern prejudices that marginalize and denigrate the importance of traditions that still provide a modicum of self-reliance and resistance to the dominant culture.

Wes Jackson elegantly summarizes the distinction between high- and low-status knowledge in the following way:

> The culture believes that we are in the midst of an information *explosion* because of the status granted the knowledge accumulated through formal scientific methods. In contrast, knowledge accumulated through tradition, daily experience, and stories, mostly in informal settings, has little status. We have taken this "folk knowledge" for granted, I suspect, for however *complex* it might be, it was not all that *complicated* to internalize. What we acquired second nature was woven in with the rural setting, the daily work, the local values and moral code. It is more the legacy of the dead than of the living. The more respected body of knowledge, learned through formal discovery or revelation of discovery in the classrooms and textbooks, is of a different order. More discipline is involved both in the discovery and in learning about the discovery. And though most of this information is not all that complex, it is more complicated for us to learn and internalize. Maybe this is the reason we assign greater value to such knowledge than to that which we picked up through tradition. There has been an exposition of formal knowledge, but what was necessary to make it accumulate so fast led to the destruction of much of the older, less formal knowledge. (1987:13–14)

Jackson has identified the general characteristics of high- and low-status knowledge, but it is necessary to take the next step by contextualizing his distinction in terms of specific cultural traditions. It is at this point that curricular and pedagogical decisions become especially complex—particularly for the teacher rooted in a different set of traditions and who assumes responsibility for making judgments about whether local traditions violate the current understanding of social relations based on equality, moral reciprocity, and other eco-justice norms. Starting down the slippery slope of colonization is always a possibility here, especially for teachers who universalize the moral norms they take for granted. Recent revelations of slave trading in the Sudan and ethnic cleansing in the Balkans, as well as economic exploitation, environmental contamination, and human rights abuses in North America, make it imperative that Esteva and Prakash's warning not be turned into a universal formula that justifies indifference to the fate of others. Again, an eco-justice pedagogy cannot be turned into a rigid set of prescriptions—no matter how well intentioned.

Regardless of the pedagogical approach (emancipatory, technicist, process, etc.), the teacher mediates how students experience and understand the aspects of culture that constitute the content of the curriculum. It is in the nature of the process of mediation that we find the specific nature of the teacher's responsibility, and thus the knowledge that should be the basis of professional decision making. When students are learning something for the first time or acquiring the language for thinking about what has been experienced before but not discussed, their learning is mediated when the teacher's self-identity, taken-for-granted understandings, and explicit knowledge influence the language that is made available to them. This, in turn, determines which interpretations will be legitimated. This process of learning indirectly through the teacher's interpretive framework, which includes both explicit knowledge (often wrongly based) and taken-for-granted understandings, also influences whose cultural perspective will be marginalized through omission or explicitly delegitimated. The inescapable nature of teaching and learning as a mediated relationship suggests what an eco-justice pedagogy should strive to be: namely, responsive to the cultural patterns enacted in the relationships that make up the complex ecologies of the classroom and the larger communities. It should also strive to illuminate environmentally destructive patterns and to reinforce cultural patterns that have a less adverse impact on the environment. In short, an eco-justice pedagogy should be understood as a culturally and ecologically responsive form of teaching.

Awareness of one's own cultural assumptions and patterns of interaction is usually gained only through special effort, such as the current effort to raise awareness about gender and racial bias. Thus, the suggestion that teachers have a special responsibility to be aware of how cultural patterns effect interpersonal communication and affect the environment has important implications for teacher education—and for the university curriculum in general. As I have written elsewhere about the nature of these reforms (Bowers 1995, 1997, 2000; Bowers and Flinders 1990, 1991), I will not restate the recommendations here. It is more important to stay focused on the areas of decision making that are at the heart of the teaching-learning relationship. It needs to be further emphasized that all teachers are involved in making decisions as part of the mediating process. It is the teacher's awareness of how she/he is involved in the mediating process and how his/her decisions affect the future prospects of community and the environment that distinguishes an eco-justice pedagogy from others influenced by various ideological interpretations of modernism.

The difference between the process of primary socialization that occurs in the classroom and what occurs in the everyday world can be found in the nature of the "languaging" process (used here as a verb that foregrounds the symbolic nature of the interaction). Regardless of culture, the everyday processes of learning patterns of interaction, skills, behaviors that correspond to the moral norms of the group, and so forth are largely done in context. The context, whether it involves learning the pattern of greeting (which includes learning the subtle and complex patterns that govern footing and framing—two essential elements of communication) or demonstrating a skill such as driving a car or tagging a building, involves reliance on others who model the behavior and provide the language necessary for communicating what needs to be made explicit about the activity. Generally, the languaging that accompanies the initial introduction to a new area of cultural experience involves a limited vocabulary that enables certain aspects of the experience to be made explicit but leaves most of the experience as an analogue pattern that is reenacted at a preconscious level of awareness. A limited vocabulary ensures that the patterns learned at the tacit level are less likely to be problematized and reconstituted. This works well in carrying out a ceremony, preparing a meal according to a family recipe, or following due process procedures when someone is accused of a crime. Other examples include socialization in storytelling, working in a community garden, a mentoring relationship, and just "hanging out." These activities and relationships may be experienced as more personally meaningful than the routinized activities of the workplace, but few individuals would be able to explain the differences between the antitradition orientation of the electronic workplace and the traditions they renew in the relationships within their community. Nor are they likely to be able to explain the differences between high-status technologies and the technologies that require the development of personal skills in ways that knit the community together.

The classroom holds the potential for a different kind of primary socialization—one that develops the conceptual basis necessary for communicative competence in addressing cultural issues that range from family and community to globalization. Whether this potential is realized largely depends on the teacher's awareness of how decisions within the context of the dynamics of primary socialization influence the student's growth in communicative competence. In addition to learning the patterns of interaction and skills that are part of the culture of the school, most other aspects of culture (dominant as well as minority, including what is shared across symbolic borders) are learned through the abstracting medium of the spoken and written word. The contextual learning of the student, such as learning the difference between work and play, watching television, playing computer games, and behavioral norms governing interaction with friends and strangers, is given legitimacy or problematized by the languaging processes in the classroom, over which the teacher should exert significant control. If the teacher is not viewed as a significant other, however, his/her influence may be minimal.

In most areas of the curriculum, language is the medium though which learning occurs—and it is often abstract in relation to the experiences of the students. What the student learns about historical events, geography, or what motivated an author depends on the language made available through curriculum materials. This layer of abstraction, in turn, is influenced by the teacher's interpretation, silence, and patterns of metacommunication. The importance of language in the process of primary socialization can be seen in the inability of many former students to identify women artists, the scientific discoveries of indigenous cultures, and the contributions of minority cultural groups to mainstream American culture. As Carter G. Goodson explains in *The Mis-education of the Negro* (1933), the language of the public school and university curriculum presents a distorted picture of the cultural traditions and contributions of African Americans to American life. Other minority groups—Chinese American, Japanese American, Latino, and indigenous cultures, to cite just a few—also identify the language of the curriculum as contributing to the widespread ignorance about their traditions and contributions. Because they were not given the language that names their achievements, they remained outside the realm of awareness for generations of students. Similarly, taken-for-granted sexist and racist patterns and their relationships to other traditions and patterns went largely unrecognized until they were named—which again depended on the complex languaging processes that constitute primary socialization.

Given the central role that language plays in framing how relationships and attributes are understood and in legitimizing certain interpretations over others, it is surprising that so many different approaches to educational reform fail to consider what teachers should know about languaging processes. Teacher education programs and education critics have become sensitive to how languaging processes reproduce sexist and racial bias, but they have ignored how the language of the curriculum perpetuates the patterns of thinking taken for granted in a hyperconsumer culture. Before proceeding to an overview of the aspects of the languaging processes that are integral to primary socialization (i.e., when students are being introduced to something for the first time and when the teacher is viewed as a significant other), I must first comment on the categorical distinction that characterizes the Freirean interpretation of dialogue.

Dialogue: The Relevance of Martin Buber's Interpretation

Freire and his followers take the position that if the relationship between teacher and student is not characterized by dialogue, it is an oppressive, "banking" approach to education. I agree with them that dialogue is important, but I find that the Freirean interpretation of what constitutes the nature and possibility of dialogue is ideologically based. Evidence of this can be seen in the inability of

Freire's followers to engage in dialogue with anyone who disagrees with the deep assumptions that underlie their arguments for universal emancipation based on a Western view of individualism and progress. The understanding of dialogue that should be an integral part of an eco-justice pedagogy has been most adequately articulated by Martin Buber, who authored *I and Thou* (1937). His writings on the nature of dialogue in educational settings can be found in *Between Man and Man* (1955) and *The Knowledge of Man* (1965).

The key distinction, according to Buber, is between dialogue and monologue, which can also be understood as the difference between an I-Thou and an I-It relationship. Each person entering a relationship makes a choice that frames whether the relationship will move to the level of dialogue or remain instrumental and largely predetermined in outcome. "The essential problem of the sphere of the inter human," Buber writes, "is the duality of being and seeming" (1965:75). The difference is summarized in the following passage, which also explains that dialogue can be sustained even in the face of divergent perspectives:

> The chief presupposition for the rise of genuine dialogue is that each should regard his partner as the very one he is. I become aware of him, aware that he is different, essentially different from myself, in the definite, unique way which is peculiar to him, and I accept whom I thus see, so that in full earnestness I can direct what I say to him as the person he is. Perhaps from time to time I must offer strict opposition to his view about the subject of our conversation. But I accept this person, the personal bearer of a conviction, in his definite being out of which his conviction has grown—even though I must try to show, bit by bit, the wrongness of this very conviction. I affirm him as creature and as creation, I confirm him who is opposed to me as him who is over against me. It is true that it now depends on the other whether genuine dialogue, mutuality in speech arises between us. But if I thus

give to the other who confronts me his legitimate standing as a man with whom I am ready to enter into dialogue, then I may trust him and suppose him to be ready to deal with me as his partner. (1965: 79–80)

Although this passage is blemished by the prevailing cultural pattern of using masculine pronouns, it is obvious that Buber understood the existential preconditions for dialogue. He also understood that a relationship dominated by "seeming" results from the obsessions of the modern world as well as personal psychological traits that intrude into the relationship. The need to impress the other, to create in the awareness of the other a certain image or to shape her/his thinking in a certain way, to use the other as a source of information, to be too preoccupied with one's own needs, to force the interaction to conform to a certain schedule or plan of action—all limit the possibility of dialogue.

While arguing that dialogue is the highest expression of community, Buber also recognizes that most associations in the modern world (with its time schedules and commodified activities) will be characterized by I-It relationships that inhibit dialogue. He further states that while dialogue is the most desirable relationship between teacher and students, it can never be achieved in the fullest sense. The teacher needs to confirm the distinct otherness of the student, trust in the unfolding of dialogue, and be a co-participant in ways that avoid manipulating the student's self-image and thoughts. Yet, even when the sequence and focus of the curriculum are set aside and the teacher moves in the direction that dialogue takes, it cannot be more than a one-sided dialogue. As Buber explains this limited form of dialogue:

> However intense the mutuality of giving and taking with which he is bound to his pupil, inclusion cannot be mutual in this case. He experiences the pupil's being educated, but the pupil cannot experi-

ence the educating of the educator. The educator stands at both ends of the common situation, the pupil only at one end. In the moment when the pupil is able to throw himself across and experience from over there, the educative relation would be burst asunder, or change into friendship. (1955:100)

The student, that is, is unable to experience the relationship from the teacher's perspective, which may encompass issues and experiences that the student has not considered before.

Briefly, there are a number of important distinctions between Buber's understanding of dialogue and the Freirean interpretation, which represents dialogue as the only alternative to an oppressive, colonizing form of education. First, Buber recognizes the realities of everyday life that intrude in ways that limit the fullest expression of dialogue. Second, he acknowledges the range of psychological problems that may impede the ability to confirm, trust, and thus enter into dialogue with others in ways not planned in advance. By contrast, the Freirean interpretation does not take account of the pressures people (including teachers) may be under or consider that in some situations instrumental relationships may be all that is possible—or desired by one participant or the other. For example, when I was seeking information in Paris about which train would take me to Nice, I did not violate the other's or my own need for dialogue. The critical distinction would have arisen, in terms of Buber's understanding of dialogue, if the person I was seeking information from had addressed me as Thou and I had responded in an instrumental way.

The selection of the effective world, in the context of the classroom, is the content of the curriculum. And it is in how the curriculum is interpreted by the students that the most fundamental difference between Buber and Freirean thinkers emerges. Keeping in mind the earlier quotation in which Buber states that dialogue may even involve showing the other (the student) the "wrongness" of her/his conviction (or interpretation), the teacher still confirms the student in ways that invite further dialogue (in its limited educational form). The emancipatory ideology within which Freirean thinkers situate their interpretation of dialogue does not involve confirmation, acceptance, trust, and the other qualities of relationship essential to a continued dialogue. Instead, if the students disagree with the teacher's assessment of what constitutes their oppressed condition—by, for example, upholding the value of elder knowledge within their community—they will be seen as in need of additional self-interrogation until they come to share the teacher's Enlightenment view of emancipation.

Primary Socialization

The ability of the culturally responsive teacher to enter into the limited form of dialogue unique to the teacher-learner relationship is only one aspect of the languaging process that characterizes an eco-justice pedagogy. The other language-mediating responsibilities of the teacher are equally important. As Peter Berger and Thomas Luckmann point out in *The Social Construction of Reality* (1967), language is the medium through which a cultural group shares its conceptual categories and everyday sense of reality with new members. It is also the medium that sustains this shared "reality" and through which it is renegotiated. The spoken and written word, metacommunication, and the semiotic messages of material culture (design of buildings, clothes, curriculum materials, and so forth) are integral aspects of the classroom. Indeed, it is difficult to think of any activity in the classroom that is not part of the languaging processes that sustain a shared sense of reality—even when the interpretations of reality are in conflict.

The aspect of cultural mediation that is especially important for teachers to understand is the inescapable nature of their gatekeeper role in the process of primary socialization. Even the teacher who believes the myth that students construct their own knowledge or waits for the moment of "self-organization" cannot escape being a gatekeeper. When students are being introduced to an aspect of culture, including how to think about previous experiences that were largely contextual, they are in a dependency relationship with the teacher—particularly when they view the teacher as a "significant other."

The connections between language and the ability to be aware of otherwise taken-for-granted patterns should be a central part of the teacher's professional knowledge. The teacher controls the initial vocabulary and theory framework (explanation of relationships) made available when students are learning something for the first time. The initial vocabulary is important because it encodes the conceptual and moral patterns that become, in the presence of certain variables, the initial basis for later understandings and interpretations. For example, the middle-grade textbook that explains that "people who work receive a salary" has remained the basis of thinking of the experts who calculate the gross domestic product—which excludes housework and other forms of work that do not involve a salary. Similarly, the elementary textbook that explains community in terms of human activity while excluding the nonhuman participants within the bioregion continues to be the basis of how most adults think of community. And the textbook and teacher explanations that omit information about the political and cultural nature of the scientific method continue to influence the thinking of even the most acclaimed scientists. While other variables enter in, there is a connection between first words and first thoughts—which is important given the many areas of the curriculum in which the teacher mediates the words that will be made available in the early phases of primary socialization.

The teacher also controls whether the language simply names the experiences and the nature of events, people, facts, etc., in ways that reinforce what others take for granted or provides a more complex vocabulary and variety of interpretive frameworks. The latter provides the conceptual basis for considering the complexity of relationships and for articulating alternative ways of understanding and acting. To cite an example that is relevant to elementary and graduate students alike: most students will continue to think about computers within a limited conceptual framework if primary socialization is in a limited vocabulary that connects computers only with progress and individual empowerment. In that case, the connections between the computer, its consciousness-shaping characteristics, the commodification process, and the globalization of decontextualized ways of thinking are unlikely to be part of the students' understanding. Some students may understand these issues, of course, partly through personal insight but more likely through a process of primary socialization to other theoretical and historically informed interpretive frameworks. The key point is the connection between the complexity of the language and interpretive frameworks and the ability to understand and articulate the complexity of issues and relationships. Again, the teacher, as gatekeeper in the languaging processes of primary socialization, exerts an important influence.

Primary socialization also involves decisions on the teacher's part about whether the language made available enables students to conceptualize and articulate the patterns of their own experiences and to connect these patterns to the different frames of cultural experience—personal, family, community, intercultural, and global trends. If the vocabulary and interpretative framework are abstract, a problem inherent in the printed word, it is more likely to lead to learning that will be forgotten shortly after it is tested. But abstractness, when combined with silence on the nature of contextual experiences within the family and community, has another effect: it sends the message that the student's own cultural patterns are too insignificant to be included in the curriculum. That is, the abstract language and theory delegitimize the students' intergenerational knowledge and legitimize the commodification technologies that are undermining what remains of the traditions of self-sufficiency within families and communities. Given the fact that this form of knowledge is given greater status as students proceed through the educational process, teachers tend, on the whole, to equate their responsibility with ensuring that students learn from an increasingly abstract curriculum.

There is yet another aspect of the languaging process that teachers mediate: namely, the cultural ways of knowing encoded in the metaphorical constructions of the words and sentences used to introduce students to the topics and issues in the curriculum. Not only does metaphor play an important role in providing the analogues (conceptual schemata or models) for learning something new in areas as divergent as mathematics, art, science, and history, it also influences the choice of new analogies. For example, the root metaphor of *patriarchy* influenced a wide range of cultural practices in ways that reproduced the analogue of a strong, controlling, rational male. The root metaphor that equates change with progress, as previously pointed out, frames how educational theorists understand an experimental and individual-centered approach to ideas and values—and leads them to an oversimplistic understanding of traditional, ecologically centered cultures.

The point here is that the teacher must be able to identify the metaphorical constructions reproduced through the language of the curriculum and must know when to make them explicit. Few teachers are being educated to recognize that there is a whole set of decisions surrounding the metaphorical nature of the language-thought connection. These include recognizing when students transform the "as if" way of thinking, a basic move in the process of learning through the use of an analogy, into a factual representation. Teachers need to recognize the root metaphors that unconsciously frame the thinking of the people who create the curriculum materials (textbooks, videos, computer software) and understand how these root metaphors privilege certain cultural ways of knowing over others. Teachers also need to be able to perceive how image words and phrases such as *data, individualism, creativity, evolution,* and *scientific method* encode and thus carry forward metaphorical constructions that made sense at an earlier time to the dominant group in the culture's history, and why these metaphorical constructions are problematic today. In some instances, it would be helpful if the teacher could point out the older meanings of metaphors such as *consumption* and *radical*; that is, that *consumption* was once associated with a fatal disease and *radical* was associated with going to the root or basic causes.

If teachers are unable to recognize the different processes and layers of metaphorical thinking in curriculum materials and class discussions, they will be unable to address the deep linguistic foundations of eco-justice issues. For example, until recently teachers did not discern the metaphorical foundation of racial and gender discrimination that had become encoded in laws, institutions, patterns of social interaction, and even in material expressions of culture such as architecture and uses of social space. As gatekeepers in the socialization of previous generations of students, they reinforced the dominant Western metaphorical constructions and became aware of sexist and racist language only when it was brought to their attention by outside political pressures. But the entire profession ignored the deeper lesson: namely, the need to be constantly aware of how language carries forward earlier forms of culturally specific ways of thinking that limit the ability to recognize the existence of eco-justice issues. The ability to clarify for students how a different set of root metaphors can lead to recognizing the possibilities of noncommodified and interdependent relationships also depends on an understanding of the metaphorical foundations of different cultural groups. That is, cultural change, as well as an understanding of the deep symbolic foundations of other cultures, requires an awareness of the shaping influence of metaphorical thinking.

There is a close connection between the teacher's background knowledge of the curriculum and her/his ability to make empowering decisions dealing with the complex languaging process of primary socialization. If the teacher possesses only the knowledge acquired from the academic discipline or gleaned from the curriculum guides and textbooks, he/she is unlikely to be aware of the importance of providing students with the language that enables them to make connections with their own cultural experience. Nor is it likely that the teacher will be able to help students examine the implications for other cultures and the environment.

Orchestrating the Ecology of the Classroom

Ecology is a word that best fits the patterns of metacommunication used by students and the teacher to communicate about their interpersonal relationships. Just as Bateson used *ecology* to encompass patterns that connect, the ecology of the classroom encompasses the languaging patterns in primary socialization and the patterns of communication that signal the ongoing shift in attitudes about relationships among students and between students and the teacher. The current emphasis on teaching awareness of and respect for cultural diversity touches on this aspect of classroom communication, but it does not go far enough in clarifying the cultural roots of metacommunication and differences in ways of knowing. Too often, multicultural education is little more than a smokescreen for socializing students to adopt the self-image, material expectations, and view of happiness that lies behind the current effort of the media to incorporate minority groups into their programming and advertisements.

The patterns of metacommunication represent ground zero in terms of how students experience domination or, if they refuse to be dominated, marginalization. The double bind for minority students is this: if they adopt the patterns of metacommunication of the dominant culture (i.e., by wearing clothes with corporate logos that communicate status and group membership and learning to think in the ways required by high-status knowledge), they will be reinforcing the very culture that is making employment more difficult for them, degrading ecosystems, and undermining their culture's intergenerational systems of mutual support.

The importance of understanding the cultural differences in patterns of metacommunication can be simply stated. If miscommunication and alienation result from this most taken-for-granted and tacit aspect of languaging, then efforts to clarify issues and broaden the students' understanding beyond the worldview of the media and shopping malls will be more difficult, perhaps impossible. How students experience their relationships with each other and with the teacher is paramount in determining whether the other aspects of the educational relationship move in a constructive or destructive direction. How something is said often becomes more important than what is said. To put this another way: the perception of the relationship may become the determining factor in the educational process, and perceptions are often influenced unconsciously by the students' and teacher's own taken-for-granted patterns of metacommunication, and by misunderstandings of these patterns.

Basically, metacommunication involves the use of social space, or proxemics; what is popularly referred to as body language, or kinesics; and tone, rhythm, and pitch of voice, or prosody, to communicate about relationships. While most students quickly learn from the teacher and other students the metacommunication patterns expected in the classroom, differences that reflect the patterns learned in the student's primary or home culture may still influence how the teacher and other students interpret her/his metacommunication patterns. A few examples of differences in metacommunication that may lead to misunderstanding and further marginalization follow.

Proxemics

The teacher who stands in front of the room and looks down rows of seated students is using the organization of social space to communicate a cultural message—namely, that the teacher is the source of control and student achievement is a matter of individual effort. There often is another message—as well as educational consequences—in the way students are seated in the classroom. A shorter distance between teacher and student facilitates dialogue; thus, students who sit in the back of the room, which they may elect to do in order to send their own message of disinterest or shyness to the teacher and other students, will experience the teacher talking *at* them. The greater distance also results in less involvement and less reinforcement. Students who view themselves as outsiders (for reasons associated with social class, peer group, and cultural marginalization) are more likely to seat themselves at the greatest possible distance from the teacher—knowing that proximity will bring them under the teacher's direct gaze and thus control. Seating students in a circle changes the dynamics of power as well as students' ability to segregate themselves in terms of their perception of the dominant status system.

Kinesics

The movements and posture of the body communicate a general attitude toward the other person, while facial expressions communicate more emotional responses toward what and how something is being said. Students use body language to metacommunicate with each other and with the teacher, and the teacher metacommunicates with students in the same way. The tacit patterns of both the teacher's and students' primary culture become important determinants of whether body movements, posture, gaze, and eye contact contribute to constructive or destructive communication in the classroom. When the student's primary culture involves different patterns of eye contact between children and adults than those the teacher takes for granted, the teacher may perceive the student as disinterested and disrespectful. This interpretation may in turn lead the teacher to repeat what was just said—which the student may experience as being talked down to.

Eye contact and head nodding on the part of the teacher are generally directed more at students that the teacher regards as higher achievers than at others. Conversely, students who are perceived for reasons having to do with gender, class, and ethnicity to be low achievers are less likely to receive eye contact and the other patterns of metacommunication that are reinforcing. The teacher who physically stands over students rather than being seated at their level is also seen as communicating a message about relationships—which may magnify the experience of alienation felt by students who already feel marginalized.

Prosody

Changes in tone and rhythm as well as pauses in speech are important supplementary sources of information about how the participants interpret what is being said as well as the nature of the relationship. Again, taken-for-granted cultural patterns may come into play in ways that undermine the trust essential for learning. For example, Ron Scollon notes that members of the dominant Anglo-

European culture share the assumption that "speech will be fluent except where slowed or interrupted by various intervening factors" (1985:24). He further observes that the faster speakers tend to view slow speakers in more negative terms—as taciturn, distrustful, indolent, uncooperative, and even unresponsive. Students from cultures in which silence is a way of communicating respect and receptivity to learning are likely to be misjudged by the teacher who views faster-speaking students as more intelligent. There are many other differences in prosodic patterns as well, of course. The overlapping speech patterns characteristic of the primary culture of some students, for example, may be interpreted as aggressiveness and indifference to the rights of other students.

These examples of how cultural differences in metacommunication may reinforce social stratification patterns in the classroom represent just part of the cultural ecology of the classroom that teachers need to understand. In addition, there are differences in cultural learning styles and participation patterns. For example, the competitive and individual-centered learning style taken for granted by teachers from the dominant Anglo-European culture conflicts with the noncompetitive pattern of learning and communicating exhibited by many students still rooted in indigenous cultures. The research of Kathryn Au and Cathie Jordan (1981) revealed that Hawaiian children have a more successful learning experience when the teacher adapts the style of communication in the classroom to fit the patterns of communication experienced in the home. Similarly, Susan Philips's (1983) study of the cultural differences between the participation patterns of teachers and students in a Warm Springs Indian Reservation classroom brought out the same point: when the teacher avoided reinforcing competitive and individualistic performances the students responded in more positive, group-centered ways. In effect, the teacher learned to adapt the patterns of interaction to fit more closely with what the students experienced in their community. We also know that there are gender differences in how students respond to a competitive learning environment—which again raises the social justice issue of treating all students the same. The problem with this abstract ideal is that equal treatment is impossible when the norms governing relationships and languaging patterns are *always* rooted in a particular set of cultural traditions that are not those of the students' primary culture.

Cultural differences also influence how framing and footing are worked out in the classroom. Framing has to do with establishing within the flow of experience what is to be the focus of mutual attention; footing has to do with establishing the status relationship that governs the interaction within the social experience that has been framed. If the footing, or status relationship, does not fit the expectations of the other participants, the frame will change—along with the other patterns of metacommunication. For example, some students may feel reassured when the teacher puts a hand on their shoulder while talking about an issue; other students, depending on their background, may interpret the gesture (the footing) as patronizing. Similarly, students who create through their metacommunication a footing that communicates equality or even superior knowledge may be interpreted by the teacher as arrogant and inappropriate—which then changes the frame to that of dealing with an inappropriate behavior.

The ever-changing dynamic of footing and framing, which represents the microlevel of power described by Michel Foucault as an "action upon an action," is particularly important to another equally dynamic set of relationships: namely, the teacher's need to balance solidarity with the exercise of power. Respecting the traditions of the student's primary culture in ways that are reflected in the classroom patterns of metacommunication, discussion at the level of dialogue, curricular focus on the intergenerational knowledge of the student's community, and even the use of humor contribute to solidarity. The sense of solidarity, in turn, provides the trust necessary for the teacher to make decisions in the process of primary socialization and in the selection of curricular issues that may, at times, challenge the students' assumptions and behaviors. If, on the other hand, the curriculum is designed to ensure the success of a particular cultural group and the teacher conducts the process of primary socialization in the formulaic manner and uses humor and other patterns of metacommunication in ways that communicate the students' inferior standing, the students will experience the teacher's use of power as oppressive. The solidarity will then be between the students and oriented against the teacher.

The patterns of metacommunication are integral aspects of the classroom ecology. That is, they do not occur in isolation from each other; nor are they generally made explicit. Aside from their largely taken-for-granted nature, metacommunication patterns are made even more difficult to interpret by virtue of the fact that students may have adopted the patterns of the dominant culture even though their name, skin color, and other physical characteristics suggest that they are members of a minority culture. These visual cues are often misinterpreted in stereotypical ways. The problem of stereotyping may also take different forms, such as assuming that the minority student who has adopted the cognitive and metacommunication patterns of the dominant culture no longer identifies with her/his primary cultural community.

If teachers are to be responsive to cultural patterns—in interpersonal communication, in the content of the curriculum, and in the commodified and noncommodified areas of community life—a radical shift in their education will be necessary. This can be accomplished only with the concurrent recognition that educational reforms must be based on an understanding of what constitutes eco-justice for different cultural groups—including cultures in other parts of the world. The change will also require a shift in guiding ideology away from the Enlightenment assumption that there are rationally formulated solutions that can be universalized. Rather, the ideology must take account of the double binds inherent in the processes of Western modernization, and must be particularly sensitive to helping different cultural groups renew the intergenerational traditions that represent genuine alternatives to consumerism as a way of meeting the needs of the community. Thus, the ideology must provide the conceptual framework necessary for a balanced critique of modernity as well as different cultural traditions. It must also foster a sense of caution in judging the traditions of non-Western cultures, particularly since so little is understood about the impact of non-Western cultural traditions on local ecosystems. We have much to learn from non-Western cultures that are attempting to recover their traditions of self-sufficiency, such as the grassroots movements in various parts of India and Central and South America. Teachers must develop the ability to learn from these cultures, as well as from the cultures of resistance in North America, if they are to avoid curricular decisions that promote solutions to eco-injustices based on ideas rooted in the same conceptual and moral traditions that are largely responsible for the injustices. This same ability to set aside what Eduardo Grillo calls the "cognitive authority" of Western modernism is also essential to learning to "read" the metacommunication patterns that make the ecology of the classroom as complex as the diverse cultural ecologies that now characterize many communities in North America.

The direction that educational reform must take, in universities and in public schools, is now dictated by the rate and scale of environmental changes and by the way different cultural groups are being affected by these changes. Still unanswered is whether educational reformers can break the hold of Enlightenment thinking that continues to privilege the abstract over cultural context, the expert over intergenerational knowledge and responsibility, and the vision of ever-expanding material progress over living within the sustaining capacities of the Earth's ecosystems. Reading the leading educational theorists of the day (Apple, Giroux, McLaren, Doll, and others in the Deweyan-Freirean tradition of thought) and assessing the current educational fads (constructivism, closer coupling of education and work, computer-based education, etc.) should make us aware that these theorists and reforms do not address the interconnections between the ecological and cultural challenges we face today. Only an eco-justice pedagogy can do that.

Appendix
Principles of Environmental Justice: Preamble

The First Nation of People of Color Environmental Leadership Summit, October 24–27, 1991, Washington, D.C.

We, the people of color, gathered together at the multinational People of Color Environmental Leadership Summit, to begin to build a national and international movement of all peoples of color to fight the destruction of our lands and communities, do hereby re-establish our spiritual interdependence of the sacredness of our Mother Earth; to respect and celebrate each of our cultures, languages and beliefs about the natural world and our roles in healing ourselves; to ensure environmental justice; to promote economic alternatives which would contribute to the development of environmentally safe livelihoods; and, to secure our political, economic and cultural liberation that has been denied for over 500 hundred years of colonization and oppression, resulting in the poisoning of our communities and land and the genocide of our peoples, do affirm and adopt these Principles of Environmental Justice:

    1. Environmental justice affirms the sacredness of Mother Earth, ecological unity and the interdependence of all species, and the right to be free from ecological destruction.

    2. Environmental justice demands that public policy be based on mutual respect and justice for all peoples, free from any form of discrimination or bias.

    3. Environmental justice mandates the right to ethical, balanced and wise use of resources in the interest of a sustainable planet for humans and other living things.

4. Environmental justice calls for universal protection from nuclear testing and extraction, production and disposal of toxic/hazardous wastes and poisons that threaten the fundamental right to clean air, land, water and food.

5. Environmental justice affirms the fundamental right to political, economic, cultural and environmental self-determination of all peoples.

6. Environmental justice demands the cessation of the production of all toxins, hazardous wastes, and radioactive materials, and that all past and current producers be held strictly accountable to the people for detoxification and the containment at the point of production.

7. Environmental justice demands the right to participate as equal partners at every level of decision-making including needs assessment, planning, implementation, enforcement, and evaluation.

8. Environmental justice affirms the right of all workers to a safe and healthy work environment, without being forced to choose between an unsafe livelihood and unemployment. It also affirms the right of those who work at home to be free of environmental hazards.

9. Environmental justice protects the right of victims of environmental injustice to receive full compensation and reparations for damages as well as quality health care.

10. Environmental justice considers governmental acts of environmental injustice a violation of international law, the Universal Declaration on Human Rights, and the United Nations Convention on Genocide.

11. Environmental justice must recognize a special legal and natural relationship of Native Peoples to the U.S. government through treaties, agreements, compacts, and covenants affirming sovereignty and self-determination.

12. Environmental justice affirms the need for urban and rural ecological policies to clean up and rebuild our cities and rural areas in balance with nature, honoring the cultural integrity of all our communities, and providing fair access for all to the full range of resources.

13. Environmental justice calls for the strict enforcement of principles of informed consent, and a halt to the testing of experimental reproductive and medical procedures and vaccinations of people of color.

14. Environmental justice opposes the destructive operations of multi-national corporations.

15. Environmental justice opposes military occupation, repression and exploitation of lands, peoples and cultures, and other forms of life.

16. Environmental justice calls for the education of present and future generations which emphasizes social and environmental issues, based on our experience and an appreciation of our diverse cultural perspectives.

17. Environmental justice requires that we, as individuals, make personal and consumer choices to consume as little of Mother Earth's resources and to produce as little waste as possible; and make the conscious decision to challenge and re-prioritize our lifestyles to insure the health of the natural world for present and future generations.

Adopted, October 27, 1991
The First National People of Color Environmental Leadership
Summit, Washington, D.C.

References

American Association for the Advancement of Science. 1999. "Science & Technology for the Nation: Issues and Priorities for the 106th Congress: Views from the Science and Technology Community on the House Science Committee's Report 'Unlocking Our Future.'" Washington, D.C.: American Association for the Advancement of Science.

Anyon, Jean. 1997. *Ghetto Schooling: A Political Economy of Urban Educational Reform.* New York: Teachers' College Press.

Apffel-Marglin, Frédérique. 1998. *The Spirit of Regeneration: Andean Culture Confronting Western Notions of Development.* London: Zed Books.

Apple, Michael. 1996. *Cultural Politics and Education.* New York: Teachers' College Press.

Au, Kathryn Hu-Pei, and Cathie Jordon. 1981. "Teaching Reading to Hawaiian Children: Finding a Culturally Appropriate Solution." In *Culture and the Bilingual Classroom,* ed. Henry T. Trueba, Grace Pung Guthrie, and Kathryn Hu-Pei Au, 139–152. London: Newbury House.

Bateson, Gregory, and Mary Catherine Bateson. 1987. *Angels Fear: Towards an Epistemology of the Sacred.* New York: Macmillan.

Berger, Peter, and Thomas Luckmann. 1967. *The Social Construction of Reality: A Treatise in the Sociology of Knowledge.* New York: Anchor Books.

Berry, Wendell. 1996. "Conserving Communities." In *The Case against the Global Economy and for a Turn toward the Local,* ed. Jerry Mander and Edward Goldsmith, 407–418. San Francisco: Sierra Club Books.

Berthoud, Gerald. 1992. "Market." In *The Development Dictionary: A Guide to Knowledge as Power,* ed. Wolfgang Sachs, 79–87. London: Zed Books.

Bordo, Susan. 1987. *The Flight to Objectivity: Essays on Cartesianism and Culture.* Albany: State University of New York Press.

Bowers, C. A. 1974. *Cultural Literacy for Freedom.* Eugene, Ore.: Elan Publishers.

―――. 1987. *Elements of a Post-Liberal Theory of Education.* New York: Teachers' College Press.

―――. 1988. *The Cultural Dimensions of Educational Computing: Understanding the Non-Neutrality of Technology.* New York: Teachers' College Press.

―――. 1995. *Educating for an Ecologically Sustainable Culture: Rethinking Moral Education, Creativity, Intelligence, and Other Modern Orthodoxies.* Albany: State University of New York Press.

―――. 1997. *The Culture of Denial: Why the Environmental Movement Needs a Strategy for Reforming Universities and Public Schools.* Albany: State University of New York Press.

―――. 2000. *Let Them Eat Data: How Computers Affect Education, Cultural Diversity, and the Prospects of Ecological Sustainability.* Athens: University of Georgia Press.

Bowers, C. A., and David Flinders. 1990. *Responsive Teaching: An Ecological Approach to Classroom Patterns of Language, Culture, and Thought.* New York: Teachers' College Press.

―――. 1991. *Culturally Responsive Teaching and Supervision: A Handbook for Staff Development.* New York: Teachers' College Press.

Buber, Martin. 1955. *Between Man and Man.* Boston: Beacon Press.

―――. 1958. *I and Thou.* 1937. Reprint. New York: Scribner.

―――. 1965. *The Knowledge of Man: A Philosophy of the Interhuman.* New York: Harper and Row.

Carson, Rachel. 1962. *Silent Spring.* Boston: Houghton Mifflin.

Colburn, Theo, Dianne Dumanoski, and John Peterson Myers. 1996. *Our Stolen Future: Are We Threatening Our Fertility, Intelligence, and Survival? A Scientific Detective Story.* New York: E. P. Dutton.

Dawkins, Richard. 1976. *The Selfish Gene.* New York: Oxford University Press.

de Waal, Frans B. M. 1996. *Good Natured: The Origins of Right and Wrong in Humans and Other Animals.* Cambridge: Harvard University Press.

Dewey, John. 1916. *Democracy and Education.* New York: Macmillan.

―――. 1929. *The Quest for Certainty.* New York: G. P. Putnam's Sons.

Dissanayake, Ellen. 1992. *Homo Aestheticus: Where Art Comes from and Why.* New York: Basic Books.

Doll, William E. Jr. 1993. *A Post-modern Perspective on Curriculum.* New York: Teachers' College Press.

Donald, Merlin. 1991. *Origins of the Modern Mind: Three Stages in the Evolution of Culture and Cognition.* Cambridge: Harvard University Press.

Dyson, Esther. 1997. *Release 2.0: A Design for Living in the Digital Age.* New York: Broadway Books.

Esteva, Gustavo, and Madhu Suri Prakash. 1998. *Grassroots Postmodernism: Remaking the Soil of Cultures.* London: Zed Books.

Freire, Paulo. 1971. *Pedagogy of the Oppressed.* New York: Herder and Herder.

———. 1973. *Education for Critical Consciousness.* New York: Seabury Press.

———. 1985. *The Politics of Education: Culture, Power, and Liberation.* South Hadley, Mass.: Bergin and Garvey.

García Canclini, Néstor. 1995. *Hybrid Cultures: Strategies for Entering and Leaving Modernity,* trans. Christopher L. Chiappari and Silvia L. López. Minneapolis: University of Minnesota Press.

Gates, Bill. 1995. *The Road Ahead.* New York: Viking Press.

Giroux, Henry. 1997. *Pedagogy and the Politics of Hope: Theory, Culture, and Schooling.* Boulder: Westview Press.

Goodson, Carter G. 1992. *The Mis-education of the Negro.* 1933. Reprint. Washington, D.C.: Associated Publishers.

Gouldner, Alvin W. 1979. *The Future of Intellectuals and the Rise of the New Class.* New York: Seabury Press.

Grillo, Eduardo Fernandez. 1998. "Development or Decolonization in the Andes?" In *The Spirit of Regeneration: Andean Culture Confronting Western Notions of Development,* ed. Frédérique Apffel-Marglin with Proyecto Andino de Tecnologías Campesinas. London: Zed Books.

Healy, Jane. 1990. *Endangered Minds: Why Children Don't Think and What We Can Do about It.* New York: Simon and Schuster.

———. 1998. *Failure to Connect: How Computers Affect Our Children's Minds—for Better and Worse.* New York: Simon and Schuster.

Herrnstein, Robert J., and Charles Murray. 1994. *The Bell Curve: Intelligence and Class Structure in American Life.* New York: Free Press.

Jackson, Wes. 1987. *Altars of Unhewn Stone: Science and the Earth.* San Francisco: North Point Press.

Kelly, Kevin. 1994. *Out of Control: The Rise of Neo-biological Civilization.* Reading, Mass.: Addison-Wesley.

Kimbrell, Andrew. 1993. *The Human Body Shop: The Engineering and Marketing of Life.* San Francisco: HarperCollins.

Kurzweil, Ray. 1999. *The Age of Spiritual Machines: When Computers Exceed Human Intelligence.* New York: Viking Press.

Lankshear, Colin, Michael Peters, and Michele Knobel. 1996. "Critical Pedagogy and Cyberspace." In *Counternarratives: Cultural Studies and Critical Pedagogies in Postmodern Spaces,* ed. Henry Giroux, Colin Lankshear, Peter McLaren, and Michael Peters, 149–188. New York: Routledge.

Leopold, Aldo. 1966. *A Sand County Almanac.* 1947. Reprint. New York: Sierra Club/Ballantine Books.

Marglin, Stephen A. 1996. "Farmers, Seedmen, and Scientists: Systems of Agriculture and Systems of Knowledge." In *Decolonizing Knowledge: From Development to Dialogue,* ed. Frédérique Apffel-Marglin and Stephen A. Marglin, 185–248. Oxford: Clarendon Press.

McLaren, Peter. 1995. "White Terror and Oppositional Agency: Toward a Critical Multiculturalism." In *Multicultural Education, Critical Pedagogy, and the Politics of Difference,* ed. Christine E. Sleeter and Peter L. McLaren, 33–70. Albany: State University of New York Press.

Mirande, Alfredo. 1997. *Hombres y Machos: Masculinity and Latino Culture.* Boulder: Westview Press.

Mohai, Paul, and Bryant Bunyan. 1995. "Demographic Studies Reveal a Pattern of Environmental Injustice." In *Environmental Justice,* ed. Jonathan S. Petrikin, 10–23. San Diego: Greenhaven Press.

Moravec, Hans. 1988. *Mind Children: The Future of Robot and Human Intelligence.* Cambridge: Harvard University Press.

Negroponte, Nicholas. 1995. *Being Digital.* New York: Alfred A. Knopf.

Nirenberg, Marshall. 1967. "Will Society Be Prepared?" *Science* 39: 155–158.

Northrop, F. S. C., and Mason W. Gross. 1953. *Alfred North Whitehead: An Anthology.* New York: Macmillan.

Oliver, Donald W., with Kathleen Waldron Gershman. 1989. *Education, Modernity, and Fractured Meaning: Toward a Process Theory of Teaching and Learning.* Albany: State University of New York Press.

Philips, Susan U. 1983. *The Invisible Culture: Communication and Community on the Warms Springs Indian Reservation.* New York: Longman.

Pinker, Steven. 1995. *The Language Instinct: How the Mind Creates Language.* New York: Harper Perennial.

President's Committee of Advisors on Science and Technology. 1997. *Report to the President on the Use of Technology to Strengthen K–12 Education in the United States.* Washington, D.C.: U.S. Government Printing Office.

Prigogine, Ilya, and Isabelle Stengers. 1984. *Order out of Chaos: Man's New Dialogue with Nature.* New York: Bantam Books.

Rahnema, Majid. 1992. "Participation." In *The Development Dictionary: A Guide to Knowledge as Power,* ed. Wolfgang Sachs, 116–131. London: Zed Books.

Rorty, Richard. 1989. *Contingency, Irony, and Solidarity.* New York: Cambridge University Press.

Sagan, Carl. 1997. *The Demon-Haunted World: Science as a Candle in the Dark.* New York: Headline Book.

Sale, Kirkpatrick. 1995. *Rebels against the Future: The Luddites and Their War on the Industrial Revolution.* Reading, Mass.: Addison-Wesley.

Schwab, Jim. 1994. *Deeper Shades of Green: The Rise of Blue-Collar and Minority Environmentalism in America.* San Francisco: Sierra Club Books.

Scollon, Ron. 1985. "The Machine Stops: Silence in the Metaphor of Malfunction." In *Perspectives on Silence,* ed. Deborah Tannen and Muriel Saville-Troike, 24–37. Norwood, N.J.: Ablex.

Shils, Edward. 1981. *Tradition.* Chicago: University of Chicago Press.

Shiva, Vandana. 1993. *Monocultures of the Mind: Biodiversity, Biotechnology, and the Third World.* Penang, Malaysia: Third World Network.

Smith, Gregory. 1992. *Education and the Environment: Learning to Live within Limits.* Albany: State University of New York Press.

Stock, Gregory. 1993. *Metaman: The Merging of Humans and Machines into a Global Organism.* Toronto: Doubleday Canada.

Storey, Robert. 1996. *Mimesis and the Human Animal: On the Biogenetic Foundations of Literary Representation.* Evanston, Ill.: Northwestern University Press.

Sylwester, Robert. 1995. *A Celebration of Neurons: An Educator's Guide to the Human Brain.* Alexandria, Va.: Association of Supervision and Curriculum Development.

Szasz, Andrew. 1994. *EcoPopulism: Toxic Waste and the Movement for Environmental Justice.* Minneapolis: University of Minnesota Press.

Van Der Ryn, Sim, and Stuart Cowan. 1996. *Ecological Design.* Washington, D.C.: Island Press.

Wackernagel, Mathis, and William Rees. 1996. *Our Ecological Footprint: Reducing Human Impact on the Earth.* Gabriola Island, B.C.: New Society Publishers.

Wechsler, Pat. 1997. "The All-out Marketing Assault on Your Child's Heart, Mind, and Wallet." *Business Week,* June 30, 62–69.

Whitehead, Alfred North. 1929. *Process and Reality.* New York: Macmillan.

———. *Alfred North Whitehead: An Anthology.* Ed. F. S. C. Northrop and Mason W. Gross. New York: Macmillan, 1953.

Wilson, E. O. 1975. *Sociobiology: The New Synthesis.* Cambridge: Belknap Press of Harvard University Press.

———. 1978. *On Human Nature.* Cambridge: Harvard University Press.

———. 1998a. "The Biological Basis of Morality." *Atlantic Monthly* 281.4:53–70.

———. 1998b. *Consilience: The Unity of Knowledge.* New York: Alfred A. Knopf.

Wright, Robert. 1994. *The Moral Animal: Evolutionary Psychology and Everyday Life.* New York: Pantheon Books.

Index